The Op

Block 3

The Wars of the Three Kingdoms

Anne Laurence

This publication forms part of an Open University course *A200 Exploring History: Medieval to Modern 1400–1900.*. Details of this and other Open University courses can be obtained from the Student Registration and Enquiry Service, The Open University, PO Box 197, Milton Keynes, MK7 6BJ, United Kingdom: tel. +44 (0)870 333 4340, email general-enquiries@open.ac.uk

Alternatively, you may visit the Open University website at http://www.open.ac.uk where you can learn more about the wide range of courses and packs offered at all levels by The Open University.

To purchase a selection of Open University course materials visit http://www.ouw.co.uk, or contact Open University Worldwide, Michael Young Building, Walton Hall, Milton Keynes MK7 6AA, United Kingdom for a brochure. tel. +44 (0)1908 858785; fax +44 (0)1908 858787; email ouwenq@open.ac.uk

The Open University
Walton Hall, Milton Keynes
MK7 6AA

First published 2007

Edited and designed by The Open University.

Typeset by The Open University

Printed and bound in the United Kingdom by Bell & Bain Ltd., Glasgow

ISBN 978 0 7492 1684 9

1.1

B/a200_Block3_e1i1_N9780749216849

Mixed Sources
Product group from well-managed forests and other controlled sources
www.fsc.org Cert no. TT-COC-002769
© 1996 Forest Stewardship Council

FSC

The paper used in this publication contains pulp sourced from forests independently certified to the Forest Stewardship Council (FSC) principles and criteria. Chain of custody certification allows the pulp from these forests to be tracked to the end use (see www.fsc-uk.org).

CONTENTS

INTRODUCTION

Anne Laurence

WHAT YOU NEED TO STUDY THIS BLOCK

- Units 9–12
- *Course Guide*
- *Media Guide*
- *Visual Sources*
- Set book: Wallace, P. G. (ed.) (2004) *The Long European Reformation: Religion, Political Conflict and the Search for Conformity, 1350–1750*, Basingstoke, Palgrave Macmillan
- Anthology documents
- Secondary sources
- Library resources accessed through the course website
- Sample historical statistics on the CD-ROM
- TMA 03

Learning outcomes

When you have finished this block you should be able to:

- understand the causes, course and consequences of the Wars of the Three Kingdoms (of which the English Civil Wars were a significant part) and the relations between England and Wales, Scotland and Ireland

- understand the history of the period in relation to the three themes of the course

- work more confidently with primary sources, both in the Anthology and online, and write an essay based on your use of sources

- work more confidently with secondary sources, using the OU library's electronic journals and other reference sources

- understand historians' debates about the Wars of the Three Kingdoms

- understand how historians use statistics and how to manipulate them using a spreadsheet.

INTRODUCTION TO THE THEMES OF THE BLOCK

This block is about the Civil Wars that divided the British Isles in the seventeenth century. It builds on both the content and the skills of Blocks 1 and 2. The religious divisions of the Reformation were still causing passionate divisions; the nature of the state was in flux; and relations between England the other nations that made up the British Isles on the one hand, and the rest of Europe on the other, were affected both by confessional (religious) divisions and by dynastic and economic considerations, many of which originated in earlier centuries. You will develop your skills in reading primary and secondary sources to analyse the content and read critically. You will see, too, how historians have used the primary sources and each others' work to debate the causes and effects of the Civil Wars, just as they have debated the causes and effects of the Reformation.

You may well know something of the English Civil Wars: Roundheads and Cavaliers, the execution of Charles I, the flight of Charles II and his concealment in an oak tree, the rule of Cromwell, the closure of the theatres, the abolition of Christmas and the great battles of Edgehill, Naseby and Marston Moor. Now that many people do not study much seventeenth-century history at school, it is the military aspects of the war that are best publicised on TV and among such enthusiasts as war-gamers and battle re-enactment societies. If you grew up in Scotland or Ireland, North or South, the seventeenth-century history you will have learnt will have been rather different.

There was not one but two so-called English Civil Wars (in the second of which much of the important action spilt over into Wales and Scotland). There were also wars in Ireland and in Scotland, where the issues were far removed from the relationship between Charles I, the Church of England and parliament, but nevertheless concerned the nature of the state, the status of adherents of different religious confessions and the economic opportunities and restraints that governed people's behaviour.

Why should we be interested in such a series of events that took place more than 350 years ago? There are two important reasons that I would highlight. The first reason is that important institutions in British political life, notably the constitutional monarchy regulated by parliament, took on the shape they have as a result of the upheavals of the mid seventeenth century, and we understand them better for knowing something about how and why they came into being. The political changes that were orchestrated in the seventeenth century facilitated, among other things, the economic changes that created the Atlantic slave trade, which you will study in Block 4. The constitutional model of Britain was profoundly significant for state building in the nineteenth century, and the seventeenth century saw the first English colonies (arguably, Ireland had become one in the sixteenth century, but that is a matter for debate).

The second reason is that, although difficult, understanding a *civil* war is important when trying to make sense of the world around us. While it involves an extraordinary act of imagination to visualise what the seventeenth century must have been like, trying to imagine a civil war forces us to confront difficult issues about our own beliefs and tolerance of those of others.

The experience of a civil war is necessarily very different from that of a war between states. The term 'home front' was coined in the First World War to denote the efforts that were expected of citizens who were not in the armed services or in obviously essential occupations, but in a civil war (or a war of invasion) there can be no such thing as a home front. The distinction between the war effort of the soldiers and that of other citizens is a slight one. The fighting might be nearer or farther, but it suffuses people's everyday lives. And in the English Civil Wars (though not in all of the conflicts taking place in the British Isles) there was no ethnic difference between the protagonists, and often what we would regard as trivial religious differences. So it was the very neighbourliness of much of the war that was on the one hand terrible but on the other restrained people from the worst atrocities; it is very striking that the bloodiest assaults were nearly always attributed to those participants regarded as most alien.

As well as the history of the Civil Wars themselves, there are a number of larger issues that are worthy of consideration: Did these Civil Wars change the political institutions to create a different kind of state? Do we begin to see a separation between political and religious allegiance? How was it possible for states to afford wars and what social and economic impact did war have on citizens/subjects?

A central subject of this block, then, is *state formation*: the ways in which the English state was challenged and altered under the pressure of the Civil Wars and the ways in which a state was defined. And were Scotland and Ireland properly speaking states? The connection between state formation and *beliefs and ideologies* is also important, for we start this block in an era when membership of the state was considered to be coterminous with membership of a particular confession: to prefer any other form of worship to that of the chosen religion of the state was effectively to hold treasonable beliefs. How was it, then, that in the 1650s Jews were readmitted to England and in 1689 it was possible to pass an Act for England and Wales that permitted religious toleration to almost all Protestants, thus recognising religious pluralism? We shall look at *producers and consumers* in the context of the development of a war economy in England and at how provisioning the war had considerable economic effects.

Anne Laurence

INTRODUCTION

In 1643, a year after the outbreak of civil war in England, the preacher Jeremiah Whittaker was one of many to note that 'These are days of shaking and this shaking is universal: the Palatinate, Bohemia, Germania, Catalonia, Portugal, Ireland, England' (quoted in Parker and Smith, 1978, p. 2). Whittaker was referring not only to the war in England, but also to the war that had broken out in 1618 in Bohemia and for the next thirty years involved most European states. The Thirty Years War was, in some respects, a continuation of the disputes you studied in Block 2, which had lingered on, changed shape and resumed, reinvigorated, at different times and at different places. In this unit we shall look at the turbulence in Europe as a context for the wars that broke out in all parts of the British Isles in the early 1640s.

An eager public in Britain was provided with a succession of accounts of Catholic atrocities in Germany, many of them luridly illustrated to show the horror of the cruelty and barbarity of acts against Protestants (see Figure 9.1). Other pamphlets dwelt on the miraculous deliveries, strange natural phenomena and extraordinary coincidences to which events in Germany gave rise (see Figure 9.2). This literature informed the responses of men and women of the British Isles when war broke out at home and, in particular, it confirmed their prejudices about the brutality inherent in Roman Catholicism.

This unit is concerned with four main subjects:

- the situation in Europe in the early seventeenth century and England's relations with other European states
- historians' assessments of the relationship between developments on the continent and in the British Isles
- historians' attempts to integrate the histories of England, Scotland, Ireland and Wales in the seventeenth century
- how we define a state in the seventeenth century in relation to England, Scotland and Ireland.

EUROPE IN THE SEVENTEENTH CENTURY

The wars that divided Europe in the seventeenth century provide an important context for looking at what took place in these islands, for the British Isles were not isolated from the continent. Travel by sea was often easier than travel over land so, for example, residents of Kent could reach Calais more quickly than Caernarfon, and, for residents of Edinburgh and Aberdeen, the Netherlands was a more convenient destination than London. Furthermore, the nations of the British Isles had different relationships with other parts of

Europe. While England, as the most powerful and wealthy nation in the British Isles, believed Spain and France to be dangerous Catholic powers and economic rivals, there were long-standing ties between Scotland and France and between Ireland and Spain. Also, Scottish trade with the Baltic had led to settlements of Scots in Scandinavia, while Irish and Scots mercenary soldiers fought all over the continent.

EXERCISE

To get a sense of what western Europe was like on the eve of the Civil Wars in the British Isles, read pp. 118–23 of the set book by Wallace and answer the following questions.

1   To what does Wallace attribute unrest in Europe after 1550?

2   How does Wallace characterise the differences between Protestant and Catholic Europe?

3   What developments cut across confessional divisions?

Spend about 10 minutes on this exercise.

SPECIMEN ANSWER

1   Wallace attributes unrest to: confessional solidarity and the intolerance of religious minorities; factional squabbling between elites; provincial resistance to centralization. This set of factors is well summed up in Wallace's phrase 'the mix of centripetal forces of Church-building and state building with the centrifugal forces of regionalism and conflicting confessional identities' (p. 118).

2   Wallace notes that the hardships of the 1590s had much longer-lasting effects on the populations of Mediterranean Europe than on those of north western Europe and that, during the seventeenth century, it was primarily the Protestant nations whose populations grew.

3   Wallace notes the survival of pre-Christian beliefs (pp. 118–9). His discussion of households and communities applies to both Catholic and Protestant regions and he notes that medieval feudal divisions disappeared in many parts of western and southern Europe, cutting across religious divisions. The kind of control the church exercised, and its ability to tax the population, was similar in Catholic and Protestant regions. Inflation and land shortages likewise knew no confessional bounds.

DISCUSSION

You can see immediately how any study of seventeenth-century Europe is bound to involve a consideration of our course themes: state formation, beliefs and ideologies, and producers and consumers. Wallace's analysis of the causes of unrest in late sixteenth-century Europe is rather cryptic, but I hope you will keep these ideas in mind as you work through these units. We shall return to them later.

You can also see that, while Catholics and Protestants regarded each other as the enemy, they both promoted faith-based societies that had much in common with each other

Wallace ascribes the demographic success of the north-western European countries to a distinctive marriage pattern. In fact, what was distinctive was that couples married very much *later* (in their mid-20s) than they did in southern and eastern Europe. The reasons for demographic growth are more likely to be associated, at least in England, with the fact that there were no famines after the 1620s.

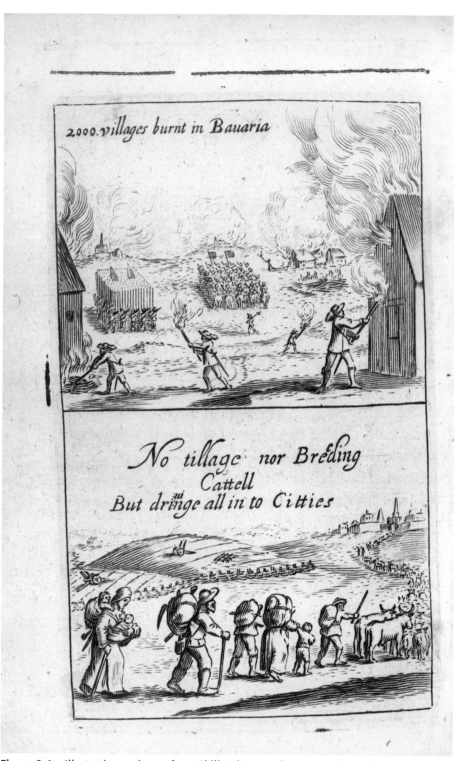

Figure 9.1 Illustration and page from Philip Vincent, *The Lamentations of Germany Wherein, as in a Glasse, we may behold her miserable condition, and reade the woefull effects of sinne. Composed by Dr Vincent Theol. an eye-witnesse thereof; and illustrated by pictures, the more to affect the reader*, London. Printed by E. G[riffin] for John Rothwell, and are to be sold at the signe of the Sunne in St Pauls Churchyard, 1638, pp. 32–3. Photo: The British Library

miserable estate of Germany.   33

CHAP. VII.
Of Burning and destroying.

Or burning, pulling downe and ruining of Churches, Cities, Villages, the like hath not been heard. The *Swedish* Army burned above 2000. Villages in *Bavaria,* in revenge of the *Palatine* cause : But their enemies spare neither foes nor friends. What goodly houses of the Nobility and Gentry, shall you there see fallen downe, or so defaced, as is scarce reparable without building new ? From what quarter soever the army riseth, they will be sure to leave some dwellings in the ashes, some in the smoake. To that passe it is now come, that every one that is a man, betaketh himselfe to armes. There is now no other aboad, but some campe, no other Plough to follow, no other imployment but the warre, for hee that is not an actor with the rest, must needes be a sufferer among the miserable patients. No tilling of the land, no breeding of cattrell; for if they should, the next yeere the souldiers devoure it. Better to sit still, than to labour, and let others reape the profits. Hence an universall desolation.

Part of the people swarme as banished in strange countries, as I have observed in *Suisse*, at

Lausan,

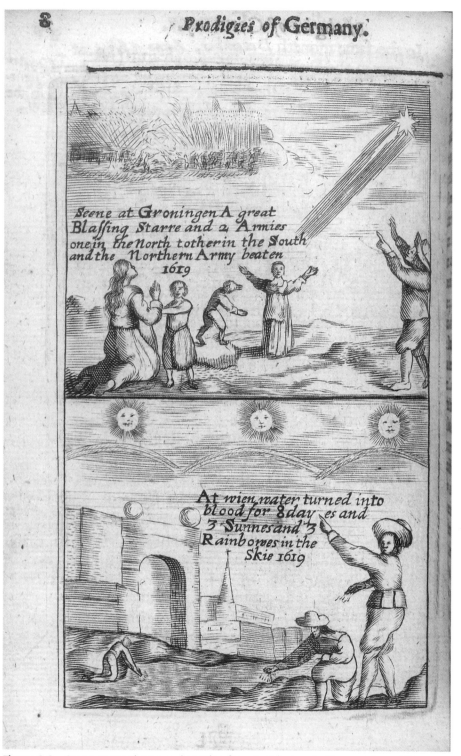

Figure 9.2   Scene at Groningen and at Wien from L. Brinckmair, *The warnings of Germany By wonderfull signes, and strange prodigies seene in divers parts of that country of Germany, betweene the yeare 1618 and 1638*, London. Printed by John Norton, for John Rothwell, and are to be sold at the signe of the Sunne in St Pauls Churchyard, 1638, pp. 8 & 9. Photo: The British Library

Prodigies of Germany.   9

In the same moneth *December*, *Anno* 1619. at *Groningen* in the Dukedome of *Brunswick*, appeared a great blazing Starre, and two Armies, one in the East, the other in the North, fighting against each other in the Heaven, so long till the Army of the North was slaine and defeated. This issued out, *Anno* 1626. the 25. of *August*, where few leagues from this place a fore battell was fought betwixt the King of *Denmark* and the Imperiall Generall *Tilly*, in which the King lost the field, and 4000. of his Army were slaine and taken prisoners: amongst them were also slaine 4. Danish Colonels, and a Landgrave of *Hessen*. Of the Imperialists lost their lives some 3. or 400. upon the place. We will not speak much of another conflict, which happened in the same Dukedome, when the fore-mentioned Starre was seen, where 500 were slaine upon the place neere *Calinberg*; nor of the bloody massacre, done by the Imperialists in the Citie of *Munden* in the said Dukedome, where 2500. Citizens and Souldiers were put to the sword most miserably by the Imperialists, the 27. of *August*, *Anno* 1626.

Two Armies fighting in the heavens.

At *Wien* in *Austria*, the water in the Ditch was to bee seene like blood for the space of 8. dayes: likewise 3. Rainbowes appeared, and 3. Sunnes in the Heaven, in the beginning of *April. Anno.* 1619. here in the same place, and City, and in the same yeere, the 25. of *October* a great, and bloody fight was at the Donaw-bridge in the same Towne of *Wien*, betwixt the *Bohemians*, and Generall *Bucquoy*: in which encounter were slaine on the Imperiall side 4500. and of the *Bohemians* some 1000. and a great many wounded, which were

Three Rainbows and three Sunnes appearing in the heavens.

Wallace, in these passages, is rather unspecific about the nature of the European struggles of the seventeenth century. You will remember that, in 1555, the religious peace of Augsburg permitted rulers of German states to choose the religion of the state provided that they were either Lutheran or Catholic (Wallace, p. 116). But this settlement stored up trouble for the future by not recognising Calvinism, a movement that was becoming increasingly important, not only in the Netherlands (as you saw in Block 2), but also in the Rhineland (Wallace, p. 146). The most long-lasting and extensive of the struggles that divided Europe in the seventeenth century was the Thirty Years War (1618–48) which, though centred on Germany, ranged from Bohemia to the Low Countries, to northern Italy and Denmark, and involved other European powers, notably France, Spain and Sweden. Like the wars in the British Isles, it was a series of connected wars rather than a single struggle.

The Thirty Years War

EXERCISE

Read pp. 155–62 of the set book by Wallace. Read it rapidly, rather than taking detailed notes, and answer the following questions:

1   As what kind of war does Wallace characterise the Thirty Years War?

2   What part did England play in the war?

Spend about 20 minutes on this exercise.

SPECIMEN ANSWER

1   Wallace describes the wars as waged for 'dynastic interest', motivated by 'political ambition' with 'religious overtones'. The account shows how there was a constant interplay between the great powers (Spain, the Habsburg empire and France) and a myriad of smaller states.

2   The Calvinist electoral count Frederick was the son-in-law of King James VI and I of Scotland and England. Because of this, in 1625 England joined a Protestant Union with Denmark, the Dutch Republic and Bethlen Gábor of Transylvania, and various imperial (German) states.

DISCUSSION

Note that I use the term 'England', for the *state* that negotiated with foreign powers was really that of England. Scotland and Ireland, ruled by the same monarch, did not have independent foreign policies. (We shall look at the definition of a state later in the unit.) This is not to say that the Irish and the Scots did not take part in the continental wars. The Scots were noted for serving in continental Protestant armies: both Alexander Leslie, the commander of the covenanting Scots army in the 1640s, and the marquis of Hamilton, a leading Scots royalist, had served in the army of the king of Sweden. Owen Roe O'Neill, leader of the Catholic forces in Ireland in the 1640s, had served in the Spanish army, as had Murrough O'Brien, Lord Inchiquin, who served both king and parliament during the Irish rebellion.

MPs in the English House of Commons (Scotland and Ireland still had their own parliaments) implored both King James and his successor Charles I to join the Protestant coalition against the Catholic forces of the Habsburg emperor, and to send military assistance to the Protestant princes. But neither king showed much enthusiasm for military engagement in a continental war.

You don't need to retain a detailed knowledge of the events of the Thirty Years War, but you do need to have a sense of how it affected every country in Europe, however peripheral. Figure 9.3 shows how extensive the war in Germany was, while Figure 9.4 shows the population losses for the period. Note how in those regions where over 66 per cent of the population was lost, there was a considerable concentration of battles. In areas such as the Rhineland, a good many of the losses must have been from armies passing through, destroying crops, livestock and commerce.

Figure 9.3   The Thirty Years War, from Geoffrey Parker, *Europe in Crisis 1598–1648*, Fontana History of Europe, 1979, Figure 8, p. 222

Figure 9.4   Germany: loss of population in the Thirty Years War, from D. H. Pennington, *Europe in the Seventeenth Century*, 2nd edn, London, Longman, 1989, Map 4, p. 587

Frederick V (Wittlesbach) (1596–1632), Calvinist ruler of the rich Lower Palatinate on the Rhine and of the Upper Palatinate on the border of Bohemia, was the leading secular prince in Germany and one of those entitled to elect the emperor. In 1613, he married Elizabeth, daughter of James VI and I. In 1619, he was offered the throne of Bohemia, which led to the invasion of the country by imperial forces and Frederick's defeat and expulsion in 1620. By 1622, he had lost his German lands; he was formally deprived of these and his electoral title in 1623. He spent the rest of his life in exile. His sons Rupert and Maurice served in Charles I's army during the English Civil Wars.

A 'general crisis', states and confessions

That so much of Europe was, in the middle of the seventeenth century, taken up by war led historians to consider whether there was some connection between these struggles. In the 1950s and 1960s, a series of articles appeared looking for common themes in the causes and descriptions of these events. Some saw the 'general crisis' as inescapably linked with a fundamental change to the infrastructure of European economies, others saw it as a crisis of the state (Hobsbawm, 1974 [1954], p. 1; Trevor-Roper, 1974 [1959] , p. 95). The debate rumbled on for a number of years, bringing in historians of many countries; more recent contributions looked at Ottoman Turkey, Ming China,

Japan and Muscovy. Although historians now do not much discuss the debate head-on, it does inform the widely held view that the wars in western Europe were a series of connected events, even though they may not have shared a single cause.

At the centre of any discussion about the mid-seventeenth-century wars that devastated much of Europe lie questions about the relationship between religious confession and state formation. Historians now debate whether the wars were the tail end of disputes that had started with the Reformation; that is to say, struggles concerned with trying to consolidate Protestant confessional states in the face of Catholic opposition. An alternative view suggests that religious issues were of less significance than the attempts of states to cast off late medieval feudal overlords (notably the Holy Roman Emperor) and to establish self-contained political entities analogous to modern states.

Studying the Thirty Years War and its associated conflicts is complicated by the fact that, when a war lasts so long and involves so many different parties, the aims of the participants change over the period. Inevitably there is no single 'correct' view, but in the next section I want to look at some of the central religious and political issues.

Religious self-determination was an important element for Calvinists, whose religion had not been recognised by the religious peace of Augsburg (1555), and for Protestants ruled by Catholics. No one talked of toleration or multifaith societies, for allegiance to the state was defined by allegiance to the religion of its ruler. (The pope was regarded as a prince who could command the allegiance of Catholics outside obedience to their territorial rulers.)

The concerns of combatants were far from purely confessional – few went to war solely in the spirit of protecting their religion – dynastic and territorial ambitions provided important motives too. The individual German princes (the leaders of whom elected the Holy Roman Emperor from members of the Habsburg family) were suspicious of Habsburg ambitions and regarded each other as rivals for territorial power. Doubtless Frederick the Elector Palatine was delighted at the prospect of being king rather than just a senior German prince and leader of the Protestant Union of Calvinist states in Germany (you will remember from Block 2 that the majority of German Protestant states were Lutheran). Bavaria was a leading Catholic state and its ruler, Maximilian, duke of Bavaria, was anxious to join the select band of German princes who were entitled to elect the Habsburg Holy Roman Emperor, but at the same time was wary of Habsburg ambitions. The Lutheran King Christian IV of Denmark who, as duke of Holstein, was also an imperial prince, was more interested in territorial gains in the Baltic and Germany than in religion (Wallace, pp. 149–50, 157–8). The intervention of the Lutheran king of Sweden was initially concerned with assuring control of parts of the Baltic Sea, but provisioning an army so far from home meant occupying territories in order to protect supply lines. At the height of its power, the Swedish army controlled vast tracts of land and the country's war aims grew commensurately. Sandwiched between the Holy Roman Empire and the Ottoman territories, Bethlen Gábor, Calvinist ruler of Transylvania, turned out on a number of occasions on behalf of the Bohemian Protestants. On the Catholic side, Spain fought to support the empire, but also to protect its remaining territories in the Low Countries. There was little chance of it recovering control of the Netherlands, but the lands to the south (modern Belgium) were at risk, with enemies of the empire on all sides.

Two states acted clearly from dynastic interest since they allied themselves *against* their co-religionists. In the early years, Elector John George of Saxony, a conservative Lutheran and reluctant participant, allied himself with the emperor and later changed sides to join the Protestants. Catholic France stood on the sidelines for many years, though offering subsidies to King Gustavus Adolphus of Sweden in 1631 and supporting the Protestant League of Heilbronn in 1633. France finally declared war against Spain in 1635 and against the empire in 1638. Under Louis XIII and his chief minister, Cardinal Richelieu, France established itself as a worthy challenger to Spain and the empire, creating alliances with leaders who would support French territorial and hegemonic ambitions rather than sharing its religious confession.

Much of Europe experienced some economic decline with rising food prices in the early years of the seventeenth century; the effects of this were compounded by the wartime devastation of trade, agriculture and manufacturing, and of the civilian population of many regions of Germany. Figure 9.4 shows the loss of population, some of which was from peasants deserting their villages and the ruin of smaller landowners, from which it was difficult for the economy to recover. The sheer extent of the war (as you have seen in Figure 9.3) meant that at one time or another most regions of Germany and many parts of surrounding states had to put up with great bodies of men, poorly fed and clothed and accompanied by enormous trains of people and goods, wandering around for years on end. There was little sense of mission in most of the armies, for many soldiers were mercenaries with scant interest in the dynastic claims of different German rulers, and still less in their religious preoccupations. In August 1635, for example, the Swedish army, consisting largely of German mercenaries, mutinied for lack of pay. The army was under the direction of the chancellor of Sweden, Axel Oxenstierna (following the death of King Gustavus Adolphus in 1632), who was imprisoned in Magdeburg by the mutinous soldiers.

I hope that what you have understood from this section that although, on the face of it, Europe was divided by confessional concerns, rulers preoccupied by territorial and dynastic gains might well set aside confessional divisions.

EUROPE AND THE BRITISH ISLES

Although the English state was not much involved in the Thirty Years War, the reading public developed a taste for news; from the 1620s, weekly newsbooks, or *corantos*, published in Amsterdam and sometimes reprinted in London, provided news from the continent.

Find, using the course website, *The continuation of the most remarkable occurrences of newes, since the 4 of June, untill this present.* Numb. 9, 16 July 1630. Finding the item through Early English Books Online for the first time may take you a few minutes; you can then either print or download it. Then spend about 10 minutes on the exercise.

1   Looking at the title page, what can we learn about the newsbook and its contents?

2   How is the arrival of the Swedish army in Germany (Silesia) reported?

1   The newsbook is evidently one of a series ('A Continuation', 'no. 9'), published at intervals of several weeks (4 June–16 July) in London; the publisher was Nicholas Bourne. The list of contents on the title page serves the same function as headlines, summarising the contents to entice the reader. In this particular issue, Gustavus Adolphus's arrival with his Swedish army in north-east German is reported.

2   Gustavus Adolphus's arrival in Germany is given top billing on the title page, but is not the first item reported inside, probably because the contents are arranged more or less by date. On p. 5, his arrival was anticipated in Silesia; further down the page, his presence in Prussia was noted. On p. 6, you see a list of forces under Swedish command.

Despatches came from many different places: Venice, Vienna, Prague, Hamburg, Antwerp and elsewhere. And notice how much of the news is hearsay – the phrase 'we understand' appears frequently. Note how many of the Swedish forces were foreign mercenaries: the Dutch (as likely to have been Germans as Netherlanders) and Scots made up 24 regiments of foot and 24 companies of horse. The 'Funnis' foot and horse were Finns. There are several references to the hardships of the civilian populations in Germany: 'the Imperialists do much wrong, and [lay] waste the country with burning' (p. 4); 'The dearth continues still, insomuch that many die of hunger' (p. 5).

The Early English Books OnLine citation says that the author is Nathaniel Butter and we know from the title page that the publisher was Nicholas Bourne. If we wanted to know more about either we could consult the Oxford Dictionary of National Biography OnLine (you will find instructions on how to find this on the course website).

Numerous publications such as this gave a curious English public news about the war. Although the government's involvement was slight, Englishmen, driven by confessional concerns and wanting to support the cause of European Protestantism, joined continental forces in much the same way that Britons took part in the Spanish Civil War in the 1930s. Some had taken part in the campaigns in the Netherlands against Spain prior to the truce in 1609. Sir Horace Vere, a veteran of the earlier fighting, led a force of some 7,500 Dutch and 2,200 English soldiers to the Palatinate, where they occupied the garrisons of Frankenthal, Heidelberg and Mannheim, and attempted to hold them against the Catholic imperial forces under the command of Johann Tzerclaes Count Tilly in 1622. There was a further, unsuccessful, expedition in 1625.

Collections of money in English parish churches and pious speeches in parliament offered help to Piedmontese Protestants and refugees in the Upper and Lower Palatinate, but no military assistance was forthcoming.

The reasons why England played so little part in the Thirty Years War relate more to dynastic ambitions than they do to confessional concerns. Although the elector Palatine was James I's son-in-law and a fellow Calvinist, at the time of Frederick's move to Bohemia in 1619, James was trying to negotiate a marriage for his son Charles with a Spanish Infanta and wanted to do nothing that might disrupt the marriage prospects. Charles, as king, took some interest in his sister's fate and, in 1636, sent the earl of Arundel on an unsuccessful mission to persuade the emperor to restore the elector to his lands in the Palatinate.

> **James VI and I** (1566–1625) succeeded to the throne of Scotland as King James VI in 1567, when his mother Mary Queen of Scots was forced to abdicate, and to the throne of England as King James I in 1603, succeeding Queen Elizabeth. He was brought up a Calvinist but believed fervently in bishops as an essential adjunct of royal power. He was succeeded in 1625 by his younger son Charles.

Historians, Europe and the Civil Wars in the three kingdoms

If England played so little part in continental affairs, why should we consider the two together at all?

EXERCISE

Turn to Anthology Document 3.1, 'Writing the history of the English Civil War – John Rushworth', a history of the Civil Wars first published in 1659, and read the second paragraph, beginning 'If you demand why my Collections commence so early ...'. What reason does Rushworth offer for starting his history in 1618?

Spend about 10 minutes on this exercise.

SPECIMEN ANSWER

Rushworth tells us his thought processes: he had considered starting in 1640 (the first meeting of parliament for eleven years) but then he realised that the events there depended on understanding 'some actions of the late king [Charles I] in dissolving four preceding parliaments'. Looking then at the reasons for the differences between king and parliament he found the reasons went back to the reign of King James and 'the causes and grounds of the war in the Palatinate', and so resolved to start his history when the war there began.

Following Rushworth, many historians have looked to the continent for reasons for, or influences on, the breakdown of relations between King Charles I and his subjects. The most powerful thread connecting the arguments is religion. The Church of England, the reformed Protestant Church that had emerged from the Elizabethan settlement (see below), was a recent creation. The Anglican Church was less a unified system of belief and practice than an uneasy alliance of people with rather different ideas about what constituted a properly reformed church, who were united primarily by their allegiance to the king as head of the church and by their antipathy to the pope and to Catholic worship. To see Protestants in the Netherlands, Bohemia and the Palatinate come under sustained attack from united Catholic powers made English men and women feel profoundly vulnerable, especially knowing that in their midst were Catholics who, since 1570, had been supposedly confident in the belief that to murder the monarch would be a religious act. One such attack, the Gunpowder Plot, had been foiled in 1605 and the government used fears of Catholic plots and uprisings to justify a policy of fining Catholic worshippers and executing Catholic clergy and those who sheltered them. The Catholic minority in England was known to have links with continental Catholic powers and the presence of large numbers of Catholics in Ireland heightened fears of a European Catholic conspiracy. Under these circumstances, a king who favoured Catholics, as Charles I appeared to, seemed to many people in England to be committing the ultimate betrayal.

This anti-Catholic sentiment was a profoundly significant force in English politics but why, between 1637 and 1642, did all nations of the British Isles rise in rebellion against the king?

EXERCISE	Read pp. 133–9 of the set book by Wallace. Bearing in mind that Wallace has written a book about the Reformation and its effects, how does he characterise the role of religion in the government of the England and Scotland?

Spend about 20 minutes on this exercise.

SPECIMEN ANSWER	In England, Wallace identifies religion with royal rule, with the legitimation of the monarch, but he notes that Queen Elizabeth did, in fact, distinguish between her roles as head of state and as head of the church. He notes that religion provided the ideology for opposition to the monarch both from Catholics and from Puritans (those who believed that the church was insufficiently reformed), but that England avoided the religious wars that split such continental states as France by a policy of limited persecution of opponents of the church settlement.

In Scotland, another form of compromise was arrived at, with different parts of Scotland accepting reformed religion to different extents.

In European politics, the Stuart monarchs' desire to be regarded as a significant power in Europe led them to eschew a strictly confessional foreign policy in favour of one that tried to curry favour with the leading European Catholic powers. This, combined with Charles I's attempts to reform both the Church of Scotland and the Church of England in directions that seemed to many ordinary subjects to smack of popery, produced articulate and well-organised opposition.

DISCUSSION	Wallace does not spell out why the relationship between the English kings and parliament was affected by the kings' desire for a pro-Habsburg foreign policy. The reason was that the monarch was dependent on parliamentary grants of taxation to govern in peacetime, even without the added expense of war. Parliament attempted to offer grants of taxation in return for the king modifying his foreign policy to support the cause of European Protestantism. And neither king would accept such a diminution of his powers to determine foreign policy and to make war and peace.

It is extremely difficult to separate religion both from foreign policy and from the ideology that legitimised the monarch's rule. James VI and I and Charles I believed not only that loyalty to the monarch (and thus to the state) was defined by adherence to a single set of religious precepts, but also that those religious precepts included the acceptance of the monarch as head of the church (instead of the pope) and that he was divinely ordained to hold that trust.

Recent historians have tried to address ideas about religion and England's position in the continent. John Morrill has suggested that 'The English civil war was not the first European revolution: it was the last of the Wars of Religion' (Morrill, 1993 [1984], p. 68). Morrill argues that, of all the discontents that the king's subjects in England nursed in the 1630s, *only* religion had the power to launch a war. He suggests we have been confused in seeking parallels between events in England in the 1640s and those on the continent, and that the English Civil Wars were not connected with the European wars of religion, but merely resembled them.

In contrast, Jonathan Scott argues that 'The crisis of 1618–48 threw not only the whole of religiously mixed, half-reformed central and western Europe into conflict, but Britain too, because Britain was part of religiously mixed, half-reformed central and western Europe' (Scott, 2000, p. 28). However, he also points out that 'England's troubles were unusual among Europe's wars of religion for being between, on the face of it, at least, not Protestantism and Catholicism, but contenders for control of the English reformation' (Scott, 2000, pp. 95–6).

Historians of Scotland and Ireland have also tried to examine the connections between the wars in those countries, religion and events on the continent. Maurice Lee argues that religion produced the ideological enthusiasm that was necessary in Scotland for successful opposition to the king's policies, though he believes, in contrast to Morrill, that it could not by itself 'galvanise enough of the people who mattered to produce a successful uprising'. He goes on to argue that 'the upheaval in Scotland was the work of the landed classes' who, in alliance with the kirk, could mount a successful challenge to the king which had nothing to do with ideas or events on the continent (Lee, 1984, p. 139). Tadhg Ó hAnnracháin makes the point that, in Ireland:

> the Wars of the Three Kingdoms took on their most European aspect because nowhere else in the archipelago had the forces of the counter-reformation established such a decisive presence ... in Ireland this reached a pitch closer to the continental experience because the distance between the competing religious positions was greater than in Britain.
>
> (Ó hAnnracháin, 2002, pp. 3–4)

What common threads run through the arguments of these historians and how do they differ?

Spend about 10 minutes on this exercise.

All of them accord religion a significant place. Morrill, Scott and Ó hAnnracháin all seem to take the view that it was religion that caused people to take up arms. Lee argues that (in the case of Scotland) it was an important element in raising opposition to the king, but that it could not alone have been responsible for armed revolt. His reference to 'the people who mattered' suggests that he believes that the support of this class was necessary for the opposition to succeed. Ó hAnnracháin observes that in Ireland, unlike anywhere else in the British Isles, divisions between Roman Catholics played some part. For Scott and Ó hAnnracháin there was a direct connection between events on the continent and in the British Isles. Scott notes that elsewhere in Britain it was divisions between Protestants that led to war. For Morrill and Lee the connection between events in England and Scotland was superficial.

HISTORIANS OF THE CIVIL WARS

Rushworth and Nalson

In the passage above, you can see that I have referred to the work of four different historians. The history of the Wars of the Three Kingdoms has been a subject of debate since the time the wars ended.

Why might we want to rewrite the history of the Civil Wars? Jot down some reasons.

Spend about 10 minutes on this exercise.

Three possible reasons are:

1   The discovery of new materials from the period might alter our view of some event, development or interpretation.

2   Historians may disagree over the significance of certain events or developments, or over the interpretation of documents.

3   New questions arise, often as a result of our contemporary concerns.

Let me comment on this list. New manuscript discoveries are not unknown and are even made from large and well-known collections. A case in point occurred in 1970. An edition of the memoirs of Edmund Ludlow, one of the signatories of Charles I's death warrant, had been published in 1698–99, when there was a revival of interest in republicanism because of distrust of the intentions of King William III. This printed edition formed the basis of the edition published by Charles Firth in 1894; the manuscript had by now disappeared. Firth was a leading historian of the Civil Wars who devoted much of his career to making sources for the period available. In 1970, the historian Blair Worden discovered that a manuscript in the Bodleian Library in Oxford (which holds one of the most important collections of seventeenth-century manuscripts in the country) was a text of part of Ludlow's memoirs before they had been edited for publication in the 1690s. Perhaps Worden's most important discovery was that publication of the memoirs was clearly designed to contribute to the politics of the 1690s as well as adding to the history of the Civil War period (Ludlow, 1978, p. viii).

From the seventeenth century on, historians have disagreed about the interpretation of events. You will remember that John Rushworth, a man close to the centre of events during the Civil Wars, started to publish an account of the war in 1659 (the year before the restoration of the monarchy). A later reprint of the first part of his Collections seems to have appeared in the 1670s in response to contemporary concerns about popery and arbitrary government. The second part did not appear until the 1680s, by which time an account of the Civil Wars by a prominent parliamentarian was rather less controversial. In the early 1680s, however, an Anglican clergyman, journalist and ardent royalist, James Nalson, published an account of the origins of the Civil Wars, explicitly trying to discredit Rushworth's work.

| EXERCISE | Read Anthology Document 3.1, 'Writing the history of the English Civil War – John Rushworth'. How does Rushworth justify the veracity of his account?

Spend about 20 minutes on this exercise.

| SPECIMEN ANSWER | He tells us that he had begun early to collect historical materials and was an 'eye and ear-witness' to many of the events he described, both public debates in parliament and private transactions of the Council of War.

| DISCUSSION | Note how Rushworth was at pains to explain his historical method: 'a bare narrative of facts', 'not interposing my own opinion', using verbatim accounts and seeking verification of disputed points.

| EXERCISE | Read Anthology Document 3.2, 'Rewriting the history of the English Civil War – John Nalson' (see Figure 9.5).

1   How does Nalson characterise his method?

2   What faults does he find in Rushworth's work?

Spend about 25 minutes on this exercise.

| SPECIMEN ANSWER |
1   Nalson admits to not having 'tied myself strictly to the rules of a bare collector', but has tried to provide the 'circumstances, causes and consequences' of the materials he presents. He professes to be concerned not to sully the reputation of a man he doesn't know.

2   He argues that Rushworth, having 'been an actor upon the stage' could not do anything but justify the parliamentary cause. He says that Rushworth does not always give the source of his materials and proves himself 'a better advocate than an historian'.

Figure 9.5   Frontispiece to John Nalson, *An Impartial Collection of the Great Affairs of State from the beginning of the Scotch Rebellion in the Year 1639 to the Murther of King Charles ... wherein ... the whole series of the late troubles in England, Scotland, & Ireland are faithfully represented*, London, 2 vols, 1682, 1683. Photo: The British Library. A beam from the divine eye rests on the figure of Britannia and an arm of divine justice bearing a flaming sword comes out of the heavens above a battle scene. A church behind Britannia burns while the insignia of monarchy and episcopacy lie on the ground beside her and she is overlooked by the figure of a Catholic priest trampling a book with a horned devil behind his shoulder

The examples of Rushworth and Nalson show how historians of different generations come to their subject with different concerns and questions. The questions that most concerned Rushworth, writing in the period of the government of Richard Cromwell and its collapse, were not those in the forefront of Nalson's mind, writing in the later years of Charles II's reign. Nalson, a generation younger, was more concerned with the politics of the 1680s than with recounting the experience of the war.

Woolrych

Let us now move on to an article by a well-known historian of the seventeenth century: Austin Woolrych (1918–2004). In 2002, Woolrych completed his own magisterial narrative history of the war. In this essay, written shortly after its publication, he reviews historians' work on the Civil Wars.

EXERCISE

Find (using the link on the course website), print out or download, and read Austin Woolrych, 'Shifting perspectives on the Great Rebellion', *History Today*, November 2002, no. 11, pp. 46–53. Woolrych was much respected for his histories of the debates in the army during the crucial revolutionary years of 1647–48 and of Barebone's Parliament of 1653. In 2002, he published *Britain in Revolution 1625–1660*, an important narrative history of the Civil War. In this article he reflects on the experience.

1   From what position did Woolrych himself write?

2   What is 'historical materialism'?

3   What does Woolrych identify as the greatest collective contribution to the history of the Civil Wars?

4   What is the role of narrative history?

5   What is the position of Civil War history at the time that Woolrych was writing (2002)?

Finding and printing this out may take you some time. (It is worth printing out this document as you will use it again in Unit 10.)

Spend no more than 30 minutes on reading the article and answering the questions.

SPECIMEN ANSWER

1   Woolrych writes of his own military experience and his references to the Second World War and its aftermath suggest that this was a formative period in his intellectual development.

2   Woolrych defines 'historical materialism' as a concern with the forces of production. In the case of seventeenth-century England, it meant a belief that the power of the aristocracy was contested by merchants and gentry whose economic power was not matched by political influence. But he specifically situates the prevalence of arguments about the rise of the gentry (one of the notorious debates among historians of the seventeenth century) in a world in which communism was pitched against fascism.

3   The numerous local studies, which were of great importance for adding subtlety to our understanding of allegiance in the Civil Wars and of the wars' impact on lower levels of society.

4   Woolrych writes with admiration of the work of C. V. Wedgwood (1910–1997), whose books vividly tell the story of the Civil Wars but without venturing into much in the way of analysis or explanation. But, as Woolrych points out, understanding precisely what happened is the key to explaining it. And his pleasure in this kind of writing (he was a fine stylist) is evident in his concluding paragraph.

5   Woolrych suggests that historians' concerns about long-term structural change have receded and that a greater role is being afforded 'human choice and human error, and ... sheer contingency'.

DISCUSSION

Woolrych's earliest work was in the field of military history. As a soldier who had gone to university to study history under the arrangements for demobbed servicemen at the end of the Second World War, he was particularly conscious of the military history of the Civil Wars. He maintained an interest in this during the 1960s and 1970s when historians, influenced by the events in 1968 in Paris and elsewhere, on the one hand, and by the development of 'history from below', on the other, began to take a close interest in the revolutionary sects and political movements of the period.

When Woolrych writes of local studies of the Civil War, he is referring to a body of work influenced much more by 'history from below' than by devotion to particular localities. For many historians, a regional study has been a way of looking at how the larger events and developments of the war played themselves out in a specific local context. Their frame of reference is national developments against which local struggles were measured.

The 'new British history': England, Scotland, Ireland and Wales

The war that split England was, like the Thirty Years War, not a single event; it was not even one war. It was two wars in England – the First Civil War 1642–46 and the Second Civil War 1647–48. In the first the Scots were allied with parliament, and in the second they supported the king. It was also part of a series of wars that took place all over Britain between Scots and English, and between Scots and Scots; while in Ireland it involved different and shifting alliances between different groups of Irish, as well as Scots and English. The wars that took place in each of the three kingdoms of England, Scotland and Ireland cannot be viewed in isolation from each other, so it is customary now to refer to them as the Wars of the Three Kingdoms. (If you want to see how all this fits together, look at the chronology in the *Course Guide*.

Woolrych refers to the impact of studies of Scotland and Ireland in changing our view of the wars. This change of emphasis owes something to the growing importance of regionalism. The press for a united Europe has given strength to movements for devolution and to the histories of those nations and regions (such as Scotland and Ireland) seeking to define their identities. But probably the most important point is that there has been a reaction against monocausal explanations for the outbreak of the English Civil Wars, in part because historians have at last woken up to the fact that the Civil Wars in England and

Wales are inseparable from the contemporary upheavals in Scotland and Ireland. The study of the Civil Wars as 'the Wars of the Three Kingdoms' is sometimes referred to as 'the new British history'.

The 'new British history', was inspired by an article by a New Zealander, J. G. A. Pocock, in 1975, who argued that:

> 'the First Civil War' is a purely English term, appropriate only to English conditions – since in Scotland there was never a civil war, even Montrose [the Scottish royalist general] succeeding in launching no more than a Highland raid of a desperately unusual character, and since Ireland had not attained the degree of political integration necessary if the term 'civil war' is to have any meaning. The War of the Three Kingdoms was in fact three wars, originating independently if interconnectedly and differing in political character – a national rebellion in Scotland south and east of the Highlands, a frontier rebellion in the multicultural conflict zone of Ireland, and a civil war in the highly integrated political society of England – and flowing together to form a single series but not a single phenomenon.
>
> (Pocock, 1975, p. 605)

Pocock's ideas were particularly developed in the work of Conrad Russell (1937–2005), starting in an article of 1987 in which he identified two common factors uniting the armed struggles in all three kingdoms: first, the three were all ruled by Charles I and, second, they were part of 'a multiple monarchy of three kingdoms' similar in some ways to that of the Habsburg monarchy. In other European multiple kingdoms, differences of religion between monarch and subjects had led to conflict, especially if the monarch had imposed, or was likely to try to impose, religious uniformity: Spain and the Netherlands, the empire and Bohemia are cases we have looked at. '[Religion] alone accounted for almost all the difficulties between the kingdoms of Britain between 1637 and 1642, and it caused enough trouble to leave very little room for any other [issue]'(Russell, 1987, p. 398).

Most historians of England now accept that they must consider the connections between the three kingdoms, or at least offer an explanation if they are not according Scotland and Ireland a major part in the narrative. Nevertheless, much of this writing is primarily a contribution to understanding the English state using Scotland and Ireland for comparison. Historians of Scotland and Ireland take different starting points and there is no consensus between them as to the significance of the relationship between the struggles in the three kingdoms.

AN INDIVIDUAL ACCOUNT OF THE CIVIL WARS

So far, we have looked at histories written by men about large generalities. But without numerous individual accounts, little of this history could be written. The consequence of wanting to know about 'history from below' has been that historians have searched for new sources that can reveal more about individual experiences and which, put together, can tell us about larger issues. But such sources are not numerous for the 1640s and 1650s, not least because a substantial proportion of the population could not read or write. It is doubly unusual to find an account by a woman. Strictly speaking, coming from a prosperous clerical family, Frances King might be considered to be closer in class and outlook to Rushworth and Nalson than to the conventional plebeian subjects of 'history from below'. On the other hand, this is an exceptional account of the experiences of an individual family. You may find the language difficult to begin with, but persevere because you will find there is a real voice speaking.

EXERCISE

Read Anthology Document 3.3, 'Mrs Frances King's account of the war and its aftermath', and its notes and then answer the following questions. I have given you fuller answers in the specimen answer than I would expect you to provide, but do go back to the document as you read the specimen answer to see for yourself how I have arrived at them.

1   What is the writer's background?

2   What can we learn from it by implication (i.e. what can we learn from it beyond the facts the writer set out to tell us)?

3   What limitations does this have as a historical source (i.e. how far can we treat it as a strictly factual account)?

Spend about 1 hour on this exercise.

EXERCISE

1   The writer was, as she tells us (line 7), the daughter and only surviving child of the man whose exploits are described – Dr John Manby, a royalist clergyman. She tells us this to establish her credentials as an educated and truthful woman and to reassure her reader of the accuracy of her account. Most of the rest of the personal information appears to give force to her account of her father's sufferings. She was born during the Civil Wars – she was a suckling infant in the early 1640s having already four siblings (line 32). The family was prosperous. Not only did her father have a living worth £500 a year, but also her aunt and uncles and her sister all had property. She went to school (line 78). She had scars from an assault with a fork (probably a garden fork rather than a table fork) (line 83).

2   Much of this story has been the subject of long-standing family discussions, telling and retelling episodes so that they have acquired a kind of patina. The element of resolution in the tables being turned is part of the narrative technique, suggesting that, for all its stream-of-consciousness form, this is actually a tale that has been constructed.

3   On the face of it, this is an accurate account, full of vivid descriptions of events that were plainly told and retold in the family with a great deal of circumstantial detail.

There is, apart from the family story, a clear impression of some of the effects of the war on people's day to day social relationships. Wright the sequestrator was despised for kowtowing to Cromwell (line 64), but note the irreverence of the woman who, asked in church to raise her hand if she supported Presbyterian church government, raised her foot (line 68). The children in the school playground had absorbed their parents' antipathy to royalists (line 76).

But there are reasons why we might want to retain an element of scepticism. In the first place, most of the events described were not actually witnessed by the writer. The letter was written with a specific polemical purpose: to rehabilitate the reputation of Dr Manby. There are both events and expressions that might give us some clues. Line 43 tells us of Mrs Manby being searched by Wright, one of the sequestrators, and miscarrying as a result. Although this is a dreadful episode, very similar accounts appear in other letters written about the sufferings of royalist clergy and, more widely, in much writing about wartime atrocities through the ages.

In lines 85–6, the writer apologises for mistakes or errors in the writing. Now this letter, of more than 2,000 words (I have omitted a good deal of the original), has been written by someone who is fluent on paper and well accustomed to expressing herself in the written word. Such expressions of inadequacy are standard fare in women's writings of the period and in writing by a social inferior to a social superior.

Frances King's description of her parents' life during the Civil Wars in England is unusual, the more so for being written by a woman. But, as you have seen, it is not a simple eye-witness account, it is a tale told for a particular purpose. That need not render the detail in it untrustworthy, but, as you can see, sources need careful handling.

Having looked at the ways in which some historians from the seventeenth to the twenty-first centuries have considered the struggles in the British Isles and in Europe in the mid seventeenth century, let us now turn to the nature of the state in the British Isles. This work will prepare you for the later units.

THE STATE IN THE BRITISH ISLES IN THE SEVENTEENTH CENTURY

Up until now I have used terms such as 'state', 'dynastic ambitions' and 'self-determination' without much explanation, but none of them are terms whose definitions are self-evident. In this section I want you to think about what was involved in a seventeenth-century state, specifically in the British Isles. Think back to the discussion about the state in Block 1, where we learnt that the word 'state' was not used in the modern sense, of a self-contained political unit, with extensive powers over its inhabitants. But, at the same time, fifteenth-century France had a distinct identity as a powerful European kingdom. Think back, too, to the elements of the state identified by Andrew Brown in the secondary source on the course website that you read for Unit 2: the degree of sovereignty (i.e. independence from an external power) of a ruler; the degree to which territories were united internally (through geography, and the way in which they were governed); a sense of common identity among a territory's peoples.

These criteria are useful, but they are of a rather different order from one another. For example, it is relatively easy to establish whether a territory is independent of any external power; it is much more difficult to establish whether a sense of common identity existed, especially after the Reformation when the religious unity of western Christendom had vanished.

The sociologists Hall and Ikenberry tried to define a state by identifying a set of qualities it required:

- a set of institutions with its own personnel including the means of violence and coercion
- these being at the centre (metaphorically rather than literally) of a geographically defined territory
- the monopoly of rule-making within that territory (Aylmer, 1990).

While the medieval historian V. H. Galbraith considered the necessary functions of the state to be:

- financial
- judicial
- administrative, including security (Aylmer, 1990).

The qualities identified by Hall and Ikenberry, and the functions identified by Galbraith, provide us with two slightly different ways of looking at the state. They are also rather easier to identify than those specified by Brown for a medieval state, possibly because they more closely accord with our contemporary sense of what a state is. Let us now use these typologies to look at the British Isles in the seventeenth century.

Table 9.1 is a chart showing schematically how England (with Wales), Scotland and Ireland were governed. There is no need to learn this off by heart; it is provided for the purposes of comparison with what is yet to come and you will be asked to look back at it when we come to changes later in the century.

Table 9.1   Government of England (with Wales), Scotland and Ireland up to 1649

	England and Wales	Scotland	Ireland
Ruler	King James I, 1603–25; King Charles I, 1625–49, advised by a Privy Council of about 20 members	King James VI, 1567–1625; King Charles I, 1625–49. In the king's absence, royal authority was represented by the Privy Council, whose members were increasingly lairds and lawyers, as well as nobles and bishops	King James I, 1603–25); King Charles I, 1625–49. Royal authority represented by the lord or deputy lieutenant
Legislature	Parliament meeting at Westminster consisting of House of Lords (hereditary peers from viscounts up and Anglican bishops) and House of Commons (1 member for each borough and 2 for each county; 24 MPs for Wales) elected by men owning freeholds worth more than 40 shillings (£2) in the countryside, and on a variety of different property qualifications in the boroughs. Sheriffs were the local officials responsible for overseeing elections. The right to call and dismiss parliament was the king's alone	Parliament meeting in Edinburgh consisting of a single chamber of 43 Scottish peers, around 50 gentry, burgesses representing 54 burghs, 14 bishops plus officers of state. Shire commissioners (about 27) were elected annually from 40-shilling freeholders, but not in all shires. (The property qualification was lower in Scotland as a Scottish shilling was worth less than an English shilling.) Business was directed by the Committee of the Lords of the Articles The Convention of Royal Burghs separately dealt with legislation affecting burghs	Parliament meeting in Dublin consisting of House of Lords (99 peers in 1634 and 24 Church of Ireland bishops) and House of Commons (235 MPs). Representation increasingly favoured Protestant settlers but there was no objection to Catholics sitting in either house. In 1640, the lords were evenly divided between Protestants and Catholics; in the Commons, about a third of MPs were Catholic Poynings' Law (1494) required that matters dealt with by the Irish parliament had to be approved by the Privy Council in England
Judiciary	Judges were appointed by the king. Local legal officers (JPs/ magistrates) were appointed by the local bench of magistrates on behalf of the king Church courts summoned by bishops dealt with matters to do with religious conformity (adherence to any church other than the Church of England was illegal), church buildings, the clergy, payment of tithes, administration of wills and morality Manorial courts dealt with matters of land allocations in some parts of the country	The Court of Session dealt with property cases; the High Court of Justiciary, with criminal cases A system of JPs on the English model had been introduced in 1609 but was not implemented and much local justice in reality was in the hands of noble and gentry landlords with 'heritable' jurisdictions, as well as burgh courts and kirk sessions	Common law courts and Chancery on the English model operated in the Pale (the area round Dublin) and in some other areas of English settlement Boroughs had JPs on the English model but little of the rest of the English infrastructure existed Early in the century, vestiges of ancient Irish law, practised by Brehons, lawgivers to the clan chiefs, survived

Executive	Ministers and secretaries of state were appointed by the king In the parishes, constables and overseers of the poor were appointed by the JPs to maintain order and collect and administer the poor rate	There was a very small executive in Edinburgh controlled by the Scottish Privy Council. Local government took place through the burghs and in both town and country through kirk sessions	The lord or deputy lieutenant in Dublin Castle maintained an administration
Foreign policy	The right to declare war, make treaties, end war was the king's alone	Scotland did not have the power to negotiate with foreign states independently	Ireland did not have the power to negotiate with foreign states independently
Defence	Lords lieutenant and deputy lieutenants, appointed by the monarch for each county, were responsible for raising militias in times of emergency The only navy was that of England	Troops were raised through landowners as feudal subordinates to the king After 1639, the Covenanters used committees through the presbyteries to raise troops	The lord/deputy lieutenant could raise troops as could the four presidents of the provinces of Ulster, Munster, Leinster and Connacht (whose powers were similar to those of a lord lieutenant in England). The oath of allegiance to the monarch could be waived to allow Catholics to serve as soldiers
Taxation	Only parliament could vote taxes for the monarch, but at the beginning of a new reign they voted certain taxes for life	Scotland was much less heavily taxed than England and Wales. Much taxation consisted still of forms of feudal dues. Occasional taxes were granted for specific purposes by parliament. There was no customs union with England	The Dublin parliament granted the king subsidies. There was no customs union with England
Church	The secular head of the Church of England was the monarch; its ecclesiastical head in England, the archbishop of Canterbury. The country was divided into dioceses administered by bishops with their own system of courts for trying moral offences and non-payment of tithes (the tax of 1/10 of income levied on all householders) Services were conducted according to the Book of Common Prayer and the church was regulated by Canons passed by Convocation – an assembly of clergy.	The secular head of the Church of Scotland was the monarch, with administration by bishops. Overall control of the kirk rested with the General Assembly of clergy and laity, called by the monarch in 1618 and 1638 Beneath this was a system of regional presbyteries and kirk sessions – assemblies of clergy and laity that ran the church down to parish level Services were conducted according to the Book of Common Order. The Book of Common Discipline regulated the government of the kirk. There was a minority of Catholics, chiefly in the northern parts of the country	The secular head of the Protestant Church of Ireland was the monarch. The church had a similar theology and organisation to the Church of England. Church of Ireland services were conducted according to the Book of Common Prayer. The church was regulated by Canons passed by the Irish Convocation The majority of the population was Catholic. There were Catholic clergy in Ireland but no formal hierarchy of bishops There was a substantial Scottish Presbyterian population, chiefly in Ulster

The table needs some explanation. As you can see, the king of England was simultaneously king of Scotland and king of Ireland, but note that each of these countries had its own parliament, that is, an assembly with one or two chambers that passed legislation and where supreme power was considered to lie with 'the king in parliament'. The Scottish parliament, a unicameral (single chamber) assembly, was for much of its life 'an irregular and short-lived event which brought together the political leaders of the kingdom to grant taxation, pass new legislation and adjudicate on disputes between its members' (Brown, 1992, p. 13). The Irish parliament, organised along similar lines to that of England, had less independence. The essential point is that England did not govern Scotland and Ireland: all three nations had the same king but separate institutions of government, However, Scotland and Ireland did not have independent foreign policies. Official relationships with foreign states were conducted by emissaries, ambassadors and envoys sent from the king of England. However, the administrations of London, Edinburgh and Dublin had separate powers to raise armies.

England had a highly organised local government based on justices of the peace and parish officers (constables to maintain order, poor-law officials to collect the poor rate and distribute poor relief) and lords lieutenant for each county responsible for summoning the militia. This local government not only kept order, it also collected taxes. Things were very different in Scotland and Ireland. In Scotland, the central belt and lowlands had a close relationship with the administration in Edinburgh and much local administration was in the hands of the kirk sessions. But in the Highlands it was in the hands of local nobles and gentry where, far from being integrated into a system of local government directed from the centre, they operated independent jurisdictions with many ancient rights and obligations – calling on tenants for labour service, for example. Something similar could be said of Ireland. Dublin administered the Pale, the region round Dublin, through the courts and through JPs, but beyond the Pale local noblemen exercised considerable powers over their tenants. In both Scotland and Ireland, the central administration had to exploit the independent powers of the local landlords because they lacked the means to provide their own administration.

Table 9.1 refers to the institutions of the state, but does not necessarily tell us everything we need to know about its functions. Unlike modern states, medieval and early modern rulers did not have a monopoly of levying taxes, for the church had very considerable powers to tax everyone, primarily by means of the tithe (in Scotland *teind*), a levy of 10 per cent on everyone's income. Should we therefore regard the church (for as you know from Block 2, European states did not permit the co-existence of different religious faiths) as an arm of the state or perhaps even as a competitor? The church also maintained its own judiciary in the form of bishops' (consistory) courts in England and Ireland, and Presbyteries in Scotland. But as the king was the secular head of the Protestant churches of his three kingdoms, he was also the fount of all justice, lay and ecclesiastical.

Look back at the criteria for a state and at Table 9.1; which of these territories seems to meet the criteria for statehood?

Spend about 30 minutes on this exercise.

England (with Wales) was certainly a sovereign state with a ruler independent of any other, and the power to make peace and war, raise taxes, and coerce its citizens. Scotland could do most of these things except making peace and war with foreign states, likewise Ireland.

England (with Wales) was certainly united internally and had a common system of government and administration or, as Hall and Ikenberry put it, a set of institutions with its own personnel including the means of violence and coercion. These were at the heart of English government, but to some extent the governments in Edinburgh and Dublin had contracted out the maintenance of order in the areas most distant from the capitals to the local nobility. As for a monopoly of rule making, if we consider the Church of England, the Church of Scotland and the Church of Ireland as arms of the state, England (with Wales), Scotland and Ireland each meets the criterion.

As for functions, the administrations in London, Edinburgh and Dublin all had financial, judicial and administrative functions, but only from London (i.e. from the administration of the king of England) could defence against foreign attack be organised.

So, it is reasonable to argue that Scotland and Ireland were nearly states, but that England (with Wales) most certainly was.

I hope that you got the main gist of the argument above. There are refinements that we might offer. Scotland and Ireland had their own institutions and powers of coercion (through the judiciary and local officials). The administrations in Edinburgh and Dublin had the powers to raise military forces and controlled geographically defined territories, though that control was somewhat loose at the outer margins. Both kingdoms' administrations had a monopoly of rule making (allowing the church to be considered with the state). None of these functions was supervised by England, but they had to be carried out with reference to English interests. For example, Poynings' Law (1494) required that matters dealt with by the Irish parliament had to be approved by the Privy Council in England. And although King James was conscious of Scots interests, his son King Charles was inclined to apply English solutions to Scottish problems.

But whose interests was the state designed to conserve? England and Wales were predominantly Protestant, with small and infrequently persecuted Catholic minorities. There was a high degree of cultural integration, though some very sharp divisions over matters of doctrine and practice within the Church of England; social status was probably the perceived quality that most divided people. Social standing and wealth were not synonymous – there were plenty of poor gentry, and noble families in different parts of the British Isles varied hugely in their wealth.

Scotland, too, was predominantly Protestant, though the Church of Scotland had a much more Calvinist theology than the Church of England, and while it had bishops, the really important administration of the church was through a hierarchy of assemblies culminating in the General Assembly of the Kirk There was a significant Catholic minority, largely in the far north. While England shared a common language and there were substantial areas of Wales where English was spoken, in the Highlands, where at least half the population lived, Gaelic was the dominant language.

Matters were rather more complicated in Ireland. There were three communities there, each of which regarded itself as culturally distinct. There were the Gaelic Irish–Catholic and Gaelic-speaking, with a clan-based society cut into by Henry VIII's land reforms. There were the descendants of the Anglo-Norman settlers of the twelfth century – mainly Catholic, sometimes married into Gaelic Irish families so sometimes Gaelic-speaking, but who regarded themselves as preservers of English language, law and custom. These Old English, as they were known, had traditionally been loyal supporters of the English crown against the native Irish, though since the Reformation they had been considered by the English to be untrustworthy because of their religion. And there were the New English and Scots – Protestant settlers who had come to Ireland to take up land grants offered to Protestants from land confiscated from rebellious Catholic Irish families in the late sixteenth and early seventeenth centuries.

CONCLUSION

Let us sum up where we have got to. Early seventeenth-century Europe was riven by wars fought ostensibly for religion but more often to protect or extend territorial boundaries and extend the powers of ruling dynasties. The British Isles stood on the sidelines, the king of England pursuing his own European project. The English state (embracing Wales) had all the institutions of a state, a more or less unified culture and a sense of identity; at its side were two nations whose claims to be states were ambiguous and which contained substantial populations who did not necessarily share their monarch's vision of the state.

EXERCISE

What weight would you give to the importance of religion in the idea of the state in the seventeenth century?

Spend just a few minutes on this exercise.

SPECIMEN ANSWER

Seventeenth-century rulers justified their rule on the basis that it was authorised by God; a compliant populace had, therefore, to subscribe to this belief to avoid treason. Rulers also associated their government with the institutions of a particular religious confession, so that obedience and subscription to the national church were closely connected.

Lest this sound too reductivist, I should say that there were many people, such as Oliver Cromwell, who had deep-founded religious beliefs, and there were many people who led spiritual lives clearly enlivened by their faith. But we have little means of penetrating the inner beliefs of the thousands of people who attended church every week on pain of being fined. What we do know, and will explore in the units following, is that many of them were profoundly dissatisfied with the institutions and practices of the church, and were prepared to take up arms to change them.

I hope that you have seen how intimately our themes of state formation and beliefs and ideologies are linked. States defined themselves according to confessional criteria, even if the realities of European politics might lead them to act against their confessional allegiances. We have seen relatively little of producers and consumers, apart from noting that production and consumption were disrupted by warfare but, as we shall see, this was not universally the case.

REFERENCES

Aston, T. (ed.) (1974) *Crisis in Europe 1560–1660: Essays from Past and Present*, London, Routledge and Kegan Paul.

Aylmer, G.E. (1990) 'The peculiarities of the English state', *Journal of Historical Sociology*, vol. 3, pp. 91–108.

Brown, K.M. (1992) *Kingdom or Province? Scotland and the Regal Union 1603–1715*, Basingstoke, Macmillan.

Hobsbawm, E. (1974 [1954]) 'The crisis of the seventeenth century' in Aston (1974) pp. 1–58. (First published in *Past and Present*, nos 5 and 6, 1954.)

Lee, M. (1984) 'Scotland and the "general crisis" of the seventeenth century', *Scottish Historical Review*, vol. 63, pp. 136–154.

Ludlow, E. (1978) *A Voyce from the Watch Tower*, ed. A.B. Worden, Camden Society Fourth Series, 21, London, Royal Historical Society.

Morrill, J. (1993) 'The religious context of the English civil war' in *The Nature of the English Revolution*, London, Longman, pp. 45–68. (First published in *Transactions of the Royal Historical Society*, 5th series, vol. 34, 1984.)

Ó hAnnracháin, T. (2002) *Catholic Reformation in Ireland: The Mission of Rinuccini 1645–1649*, Oxford, Oxford University Press.

Parker, G. and Smith, L. (1978) 'Introduction' in Parker, G. and Smith, L. (eds) *The General Crisis of the Seventeenth Century*, London, Routledge and Kegan Paul, pp. 1–25.

Pocock, J.G.A. (1975) 'British history: a plea for a new subject', *Journal of Modern History*, vol. 47, pp. 601–21.

Russell, C. (1987) 'The British problem and the English civil war', *History*, vol. 72, pp. 395–415.

Scott, J. (2000) *England's Troubles: Seventeenth-Century English Political Instability in European Context*, Cambridge, Cambridge University Press.

Trevor-Roper, H. (1974 [1959]) 'The general crisis of the seventeenth century' in Aston (1974), pp. 59–95. (First published in *Past and Present*, no. 16, 1959.)

Anne Laurence

INTRODUCTION

On 22 August 1642, King Charles I raised his standard at Nottingham and effectively initiated war. This curiously archaic event (which was to feature in the depositions taken from witnesses at his trial (see Anthology Document 3.17, 'The trial of Charles first, 1649', part (b) 'Depositions taken against the king') came as the culmination of a series of events and developing ideas that involved far more than the king's relations with the parliament at Westminster and his English and Welsh subjects' objections to the devices he had used to govern for eleven years without parliament. As we shall be dealing with a series of complex events across the three kingdoms, you will find it useful to have the chronology given in the *Course Guide* to hand.

So, in this unit we shall concentrate on the following subjects:

- the developments in the British Isles that led to the outbreak of war
- the debates between historians about the causes of the wars
- how to use evidence from church records to learn about changes in religion and society.

A civil war poses particular challenges to the idea of the state; indeed, it would seem to suggest that the state had broken down since the monopoly of rule making is contested. Yet for a civil war to continue, many of the institutions of a state have to be sustained. Wars need money, so the revenue-raising functions of the state are essential, as are the means of violence and coercion. So financial functions and administrative functions need to persist. It will become clear to you that beliefs were at the very core of the reasons why people went to war: differing visions of the church inflamed passions to the point that people were prepared to kill each other. At the same time, the king, fixed to a single ideology of rule (that he held his power from God alone and that no earthly power might restrict it), found that his subjects were developing other ideas. We shall see how the economic interests of a particular set of producers (lead miners) influenced their political allegiances.

THINKING ABOUT CAUSES

Identifying causes

Historians are in the habit of referring to 'pre-Civil War England' as if everyone in the 1630s knew what was about to happen. There were certainly signs that the relations between the king and a significant number of his most influential subjects had deteriorated. But to what extent did events of King Charles's reign and, in particular, the period 1629–40 when he governed without parliament – or, indeed, earlier developments – point inexorably to the breakdown of relations between ruler and ruled? Identifying the inevitability of civil war is not the same thing as identifying long-term causes, for how do we distinguish between a pre-existing event (i.e. something that simply happened to occur earlier) and a cause (i.e. something that materially contributed to a later event)?

We need to do an exercise in common sense. Here is a list of events that preceded Charles I raising his standard at Nottingham in 1642:

- 1536–39: dissolution of the religious houses (monasteries and nunneries) and appropriation of their property by the king
- 1558: accession of Queen Elizabeth to the throne of England
- 1588: defeat of the Spanish Armada
- 1603: accession of James VI of Scotland to the throne of England as King James I
- 1625: accession of Charles I.

Can we say that these events caused war to break out in 1642? To do this we have to explain *how* they did so. Let us take the example of the dissolution of the religious houses following the Reformation. Some historians have argued that, because this led to a free land market, the old monopoly of access to government by an aristocracy whose power arose from their territorial holdings was broken. Men who had done well as lawyers, civil servants and MPs acquired landed estates and were hungry for power. The consistent refusal of successive monarchs to give them political influence by offering them the prestigious offices that they felt their wealth and property warranted created a class of people disposed to challenge the monarch's powers. This argument has been put in a variety of different ways by different historians and has some strengths. But let us look more closely at what we would have to do to establish that the dissolution of the religious houses actually *was* a cause.

1 Note the time difference. Over 100 years elapsed between the dissolution and the outbreak of civil war, so the individuals who received the lands were long dead; possibly the grandchildren of the original recipients of the former monastic lands might be involved. So we need to establish whether the land market continued to be fluid or whether there was a flurry of activity for a period (it would be useful to establish what period) with the market then settling down.

2 What evidence is there that the increase in the amount of land for sale (which is incontrovertible) led to it being acquired by a different kind of person? In other words, how do we know that existing landowners did not simply use the market as a means of consolidating their already large land-holdings?

3 For what purpose did Henry VIII use the monastic lands? Was this a case of privatising a national asset for cash or services?

4 Were these new men excluded from office and were they aggrieved? And if so, did they continue to be aggrieved for eighty years?

The historian Lawrence Stone (1919–1999), one of the exponents of the idea that the causes of the Civil Wars lay in the distant past, believed that there was a shift of wealth away from church, crown and the old aristocracy and towards people he describes as 'upper middle and middle classes'. He suggested that the reasons for this shift were the improvidence of the old rich and the entrepreneurial activities of the new rich. But he also argued that the rise of Puritanism and the spread of education encouraged the rising middle class to challenge the traditional wielders of power (Stone, 1972, pp. 75–6). To establish all these things suggests a formidable research programme and one to which Stone was more than equal. His work on the composition and wealth of the gentry and aristocracy showed how the aristocracy was declining, while his work on education showed how the rising men of the middling sort equipped themselves for challenging the traditional elite (Stone, 1965, 1974; Stone and Stone, 1984).

Looking at the rest of my list, it would be difficult to argue that Elizabeth's accession by itself could be the cause of a civil war eighty years later; it did have important consequences, though, particularly in guaranteeing a Protestant monarchy (a problem for Ireland). And Elizabeth's reign as a whole, once she proved to be childless, assured the union of crowns with Scotland since her heir was its Protestant king, James VI. The settlement that she agreed, when the church was re-protestantised following the death of the Catholic Queen Mary Tudor, left much unfinished business for those members of the Church of England who believed that further reform in a Protestant direction was important. (This is dealt with briefly on pp. 133–5 of Wallace.) A good deal of this unfinished business surfaced under the pressure of Charles I's attempts to reform the church in what seemed to be a *less* Protestant direction.

We could make similar comments about the other events, but I hope that you can see that ascribing causes involves establishing a direct association between one event and another. That one event or idea precedes another does not necessarily create a causal connection. I emphasise the need to explain *why* one thing caused another.

It is very much easier to see direct connections between events more closely related in time to the outbreak of war but merely being proximate in time still does not create a direct causal connection. So, if we want to say that the accession of Charles I in 1625 was a cause of civil war breaking out in 1642, we would need to explain *how* it contributed. In the next section we shall look at the events of Charles's reign and at their contribution to the breakdown of relations between the king and his subjects.

Charles I, second son of James VI of Scotland and I of England, was born in Scotland in 1600. His elder glamorous, learned and athletic brother, Henry, had died in 1612. James, anxious to cut a dash in European politics, wanted to negotiate a marriage for Charles, now the heir, with the king of Spain's daughter. When negotiations collapsed, Charles looked to France and, shortly after his accession to the throne in 1625, married Henrietta Maria, daughter of the French king, Henri IV. Her devout Catholicism and her strong influence over her husband led to suspicions that the king himself was moving towards Catholicism.

HOW DID RELATIONS BETWEEN THE KING AND HIS SUBJECTS BREAK DOWN?

Charles I and the eleven years' personal rule in England and Wales

Charles I succeeded as king on James I's death in 1625. James had resented parliament's demands for power over royal policy, but realised that he could not govern, even in peacetime, on the income he had. The monarch was expected to pay for the conduct of government from a variety of sources, which included both income from lands she or he held personally and taxes granted by parliament. So masques, mistresses, secretarial expenses, pensions for clients, bribes to foreign princes, wages for court officials and soldiers, the purchase of arms and equipment, and salaries for spies all came out of the same account. But James had learnt political skills during the difficult years when, as king of Scotland in place of his deposed mother Mary Stuart (Queen of Scots), he had had to negotiate with competing factions. Temperamentally, Charles was a very different character: inflexible, uncompromising, brooking no criticism, conscious of his dignity, decorous, uxorious, religious and a great collector of Renaissance art. Even his loyal subject Edward Hyde, the earl of Clarendon, said of him:

> His kingly virtues had some mixture and allay that hindered them from shining in full lustre, and from producing those fruits they should have been attended with ...

> He was very fearless in his person, but not enterprising; and had an excellent understanding, but was not confident enough of it; which made him oftentimes change his own opinion for a worse, and follow the advice of a man that did not judge so well as himself.
>
> (Clarendon, 1888, vol. 4, p. 490)

As king, he had three main concerns in England and Wales: how to fund his government, how to limit parliament's interference in his rule and how to reform the church. He showed remarkably little interest in his other two kingdoms, Scotland and Ireland.

Financing government

As was usual for a new monarch, Charles called a parliament, expecting that it would, as parliaments had previously done, grant him for life the income from tonnage and poundage (customs dues whose rate could be set by the monarch). His expenses were high. Apart from the usual costs of administration, he had funded an unsuccessful expedition to defend the Palatinate in 1625 and was committed to spending £20,000 a month supporting the Danes in the Thirty Years War (see Unit 9, pp. 19–20). But parliament, fearful of his war strategy and unhappy about his proposal to take a Catholic wife, granted the king tonnage and poundage for one year only, though they also granted two subsidies (a form of direct tax, about £100,000). Customs dues (of which tonnage and poundage were a substantial part) typically formed about 30 per cent of government income. These sources of finance, together with the king's other revenues, came to far less than he needed to run the government in peacetime, let alone one which was engaged on foreign military ventures. Not content with his intervention in Germany, he allowed his favourite, the duke of Buckingham, to lead one expedition against Spain and another to support the French Protestant Huguenot rebels at La Rochelle, both of which were military disasters for the English.

So, from the earliest days of his reign, Charles was looking for ways to raise revenue. Each of the parliaments of 1625, 1626 and 1628 tried to exact concessions from him in exchange for grants of money, but he was utterly opposed to the idea of bargaining with his subjects. In 1629, he dissolved his third parliament and looked for alternative sources of income. In the ensuing eleven years without parliament he proved surprisingly successful by, as the historian John Kenyon put it, 'probing the wall of law and custom which protected his subjects' purses, hoping to find a gap through which he could press' (Kenyon, 1986, p. 52). In the absence of parliament, his subjects had to find other ways of expressing their opposition to his personal rule.

EXERCISE

Look at Table 10.1. The left-hand column lists the king's chief revenue-raising activities. The right-hand column lists challenges to the king.

1   What common features do you notice about the sources of revenue?

2   How did the king's subjects challenges his policies?

Spend about 15 minutes on this exercise.

Table 10.1   Sources of revenue and challenges to them

Sources of royal revenue	Challenges
Forced loans	
A medieval device, used by both Elizabeth and James I, whereby the monarch could solicit loans from the general public in case of threat. It was understood that there was no real prospect of repayment. Charles ordered one in 1626 (which raised £243,000)	In 1626, the legality of forced loans was challenged by judges In 1627, large numbers of gentlemen refused to subscribe, were summoned to London and imprisoned. In the 'five knights case', five of them demanded that judges adjudicate the legality of their detention (not of the loan). The judges decided for the king by a narrow margin
Tonnage and poundage	
Granted to the king for 12 months in 1625, he continued to levy the tax. After 1641, all customs dues were controlled by parliament	Richard Chambers, a merchant, refused to pay tonnage and poundage in 1629, claiming in court that 'the merchants are in no part of the world so screwed and wrung as in England' (Tawney, 1928, p. 74). He was fined £2,000 for scandalous words and committed to the Fleet prison, where he remained for six years
Knighthood fines	
In 1630, Charles revived a device dating from Henry III's reign under which owners of estates worth £40 a year or more had to present themselves at the coronation in 1625 to be knighted. Those who had not claimed it had to pay a fee. Abolished in 1641	Of particular importance to county gentry, many of whom refused, some claiming they had not been worth £40 in 1625. Edward Stephens of Gloucestershire brought an action in the Court of Exchequer, arguing he had not been summoned in 1626. The court found for the king
Forest laws	
From 1634, attempts were made to revive the king's right to any land that had once been forest. In 1642, forest boundaries were defined, closing this source of revenue, but the laws were not repealed	Of particular importance to families with larger landed estates, though much former royal forest was regarded as common land
Monopolies	
In 1632, the granting of a patent to a corporation for the manufacture of soap exploited a loophole in the 1624 Act abolishing the king's right to grant individuals the right to a commercial monopoly over a trade or manufacturing process. Monopolies encouraged domestic innovation, regulated trade and discouraged competition, but also provided the crown with revenue	Outcry against the tax referred to 'popish soap'. Other monopolies were established on salt, coals and starch

Wardship and purveyance

The Court of Wards administered the estates of heirs below the age of majority and could choose their marriage partners. From Elizabeth's time, wardships of wealthy children were sold. The court was abolished in 1646

Purveyance was the right of the royal household to buy provisions at cost price, and was abolished in 1660

Both exactions had been regarded as abuses from Queen Elizabeth's time

Ship Money

This tax had formerly been levied on maritime counties to provide defences in time of war or threat of war. Charles extended the levy to inland counties. Declared illegal in 1642

Legal queries in 1635 and 1636 produced a judgement that the king was entitled to levy the tax. In 1637, John Hampden was prosecuted for debt for not paying Ship Money. The judges found 7:5 in favour of the king

SPECIMEN ANSWER

1   They were all existing measures. The king did not introduce new taxes, but adapted ancient ways of raising revenue.

2   Without parliament sitting, the king's opponents had to use the law courts to challenge his policies, especially to contest his right to levy extra-parliamentary taxation.

DISCUSSION

This antiquarianism was quite self-conscious. Sir John Borough, keeper of the records in the Tower of London, was commissioned to research methods used by earlier monarchs to raise money. Many of the devices he came up with exploited rights that had fallen into disuse. Knighthood fines proved to be one of the largest sources of revenue in the period 1625–35. Michael Braddick describes them as, on the one hand, 'fiscal feudalism' (forest and knighthood fines, wardship, monopolies) – that is to say rights that derived from the king's historic position as tenant-in-chief at the summit of the feudal system – and, on the other, prerogative taxes (Ship Money, purveyance, forced loans), the right to levy which arose as a consequence of the personal powers of the monarch (Braddick, 1996, pp. 72–88).

EXERCISE

Read Anthology Document 3.4, 'Resistance to Ship Money'. What do you notice about the people who refused to pay Ship Money in the parish of Harrow?

Spend about 10 minutes on this exercise.

SPECIMEN ANSWER

The poverty of some of those required to pay is striking – Mrs Miller had a single piece of cloth seized.

DISCUSSION

This document shows how widespread and violent the opposition to Ship Money could be. Forty people in a single parish seems a large number of objectors (though we do not know how large the parish was). It is striking how poor some of the tax-paying public was. Women could be householders (they were usually widows, occasionally spinsters) and were liable for taxes, but had none of the political rights of a householder.

John Hampden (1594–1643), a Buckinghamshire MP, in 1627 refused to pay a forced loan and in 1635 refused to pay Ship Money. A leading member of the Short and Long Parliaments, he was one of the five MPs the king attempted to arrest in 1642. He raised a regiment of foot for parliament in 1642 and was killed at the battle of Chalgrove.

While the objections of poorer people might have been an irritation to the king and his officials, a more significant challenge was mounted in the law courts when the Buckinghamshire gentleman and former MP, John Hampden, refused to pay and was prosecuted for debt. Of twelve judges, seven found for the crown. One of the dissenting judges, Sir Robert Berkeley, extended his consideration far beyond the simple matter of a country gentleman's unpaid bill and used the occasion to declare that the king's subjects 'have a birthright in the laws of the kingdom. No new laws can be put upon them, none of their laws can be altered or abrogated, without common consent in parliament' (quoted in Kenyon, 1986, p. 100).

Cases challenging the king's right to levy extra-parliamentary taxation brought up such broad constitutional issues as the king's right to order a subject's imprisonment and the distinction between the king's ordinary and emergency powers. In turn this led to conflict between the king and the judiciary, and Lord Justice Crew was dismissed in 1626 for refusing to admit the legality of the forced loan.

As well finding new sources of income, royal officials tried to make tax collection more efficient – a policy especially promoted under the name of 'the policy of thorough' by Charles's close allies the archbishop of Canterbury, William Laud, and the president of the Council of the North, Thomas Wentworth. 'Nowadays the uttermost that all his Majesty's ministers can do scarcely restrains the people within the bounds of respect and obedience' claimed Wentworth, setting himself the mission to reverse this (Sharpe, 1992, p. 135).

Thomas Wentworth, earl of Strafford (1593–1641), a Yorkshire gentleman and MP, had been a leading opponent of the king's policies in the 1620s. Appointed lord president of the Council of the North by the king in 1628, he went to Ireland in 1633 as deputy lieutenant, where he tried to reform both the Church of Ireland and the government's finances. He was created earl of Strafford and promoted to lord lieutenant (a change of title rather than of role) in 1640. He was tried by parliament for his part in encouraging the king to use an army against his subjects and executed in 1641.

William Laud (1573–1645) was president of St John's College, Oxford, and vice-chancellor of the university. Appointed successively bishop of St David's, Bath and Wells, and London, he became archbishop of Canterbury in 1632. He wanted to make Anglican worship more reverential, to reinstate ceremony and to emphasise the sanctity of the sacraments. To improve the quality of the clergy, he tried to raise clerical incomes by recovering ecclesiastical property and revenues that had passed to lay people. He aspired to extend English forms of worship to Scotland. As one of the king's most influential advisers in the 1630s, he was impeached and executed in 1645.

The unpopularity both of the fiscal devices used by the king and of his counsellors consolidated opposition to the king. Many of his subjects, forced now to use the law courts to challenge royal policy in the absence of parliament, began seriously to question whether a state in which all powers flowed from the king was sustainable. Yet the king's opponents shared many of his values and attitudes.

EXERCISE

Turn now to the *Visual Sources*, Plate 10.1, and look at the portraits by Van Dyck. You already have some biographical information about the king, Laud and Wentworth. Robert Rich, second earl of Warwick (1587–1658) had been a courtier, but during the 1620s distanced himself from the royal court and allied himself with the Puritan opposition. He opposed the forced loans, Ship Money and extension of the forest laws. How might historians use paintings such as these?

Spend about 5 minutes on this exercise.

SPECIMEN ANSWER

The paintings suggest that all the subjects shared a common culture. Their attitudes, clothing and props suggest men of authority and culture. Yet the earl of Warwick was from the 1620s a significant opponent of the king and his ministers. We cannot deduce from someone's appearance which side they supported.

Anthony Van Dyke (1599–1641), a Flemish painter, was the king's favourite portraitist (he was knighted in 1638); he painted many members of the court and nobility. Most of his non-royal portraits were of people who supported the king in the Civil Wars, but he also painted aristocratic opponents of the king, such as the earl of Warwick.

The church

Apart from concerns about the propriety of the king governing without parliament and conducting a foreign policy allying him with the Catholic powers of Europe, his subjects harboured deep suspicions about his attitude to the Church of England, of which he was head. Many of them, clerical and lay, believed that the Elizabethan church settlement had not created a sufficiently Protestant church, and that the Church of England was in urgent need of reform. Attendance at church services was compulsory and non-attenders could be fined; it was illegal to hold or attend services outside the church. Reformers faced a king who believed that his kingship was derived from God, that Anglican (Church of England) bishops were the direct spiritual descendants of Christ's apostles, and that dissent from the beliefs and ceremonies of the church amounted to treason. Even to question these beliefs and practices was to arouse the king's displeasure, and there was a formidable array of devices at his command to enforce conformity. In particular, there were the prerogative courts of Star Chamber and High Commission, which were able to impose severe penalties on dissidents such as William Prynne, Henry Burton and John Bastwick who, in 1637, were branded with hot irons and had their ears cropped for publishing pamphlets against the government of the church by bishops (episcopacy). There was something noble about the men, and they became popular heroes, but they were, in their own ways, just as unmoving as the king.

If the king's subjects were unhappy with his religious views at the start of his reign, his policies did nothing to win them over. In 1632, he appointed as archbishop of Canterbury William Laud, who owed his rapid career advancement to the king's confidence in him (see p. 138 of the set book by Wallace). Laud, like the king, was not a convinced predestinarian; both men inclined to the views of the Dutch theologian Jacob Arminius, who argued that individual believers' salvation was not foreordained), this made his appointment extremely controversial. But Laud's primary concern was with the decorous conduct of religious services in surroundings that would inspire congregations with the presence of God. As archbishop, he extended the programme of rebuilding churches (many of which were in a considerable state of disrepair); most noteworthy was the restoration of old St Paul's Cathedral (see Figure 10.1) under the direction of the king's surveyor, Inigo Jones. This concern with the externals of worship convinced those who wanted reform in a more Protestant direction that the king and his archbishop were leading the church in the opposite direction, towards a form of Catholicism.

Laud himself believed that he was enforcing existing measures that had long been flouted. The rules governing the church, the canons, last revised in 1604, specified in some detail how churches were to be furnished and equipped. Laud set about ensuring that every church conformed to the canons, and parish officials were authorised to acquire missing items, such as prayer books or coverings for the communion table. During the 1630s, he reported to the king, for example, that 'the greatest part of Wiltshire [is] overgrown with the humours of those men that do not conform' and that religious radicals in Ashford, Kent 'put a great many simple people, especially women, into great distemper against the church' (Laud, 1847–60, vol. 5, part 2, pp. 324, 347). To carry out his reforms, however, the archbishop needed an effective episcopate. He believed in the apostolic succession of bishops (that they were descended by the laying on of hands in a continuous line from Christ's apostles) and the

Figure 10.1 Wenceslaus Hollar, *Old St Paul's from the East after Restoration*. Photo: Guildhall Library, City of London

spiritual authority that this descent conferred, but he also saw them as the church's executive arm, through whom any changes might be effected and lax observance of existing regulations tightened up.

The real change came with Laud's injunctions of 1637. Since the early days of Elizabeth's reign, the communion table had been positioned in the centre of the chancel in such a way that communicants could gather round it (as you have seen at Hailes church on DVD 1). Instead, the injunctions now required that the communion table be removed to the upper end of the chancel, placed along the east wall, and railed off. Plate 10.2 in the *Visual Sources* shows the communion table (4) set against the east wall and raised up on steps, behind rails (5). The two positions represented fundamental differences of attitude to the place of the sacraments in Christian worship. For Puritans, following the practice of the Elizabethan church, the bread and the wine of the communion service *commemorated* Christ's last supper and were to be treated respectfully, but were to be taken communally as a symbol of Christ's role as saviour. For the king, Archbishop Laud and their supporters, the sacraments were to be revered, to be received by *kneeling* communicants before the altar representing Christ's sacrifice, a symbolic position that horrified Puritans.

Laud used his powers as archbishop to try to secure uniformity of practice in the church. In particular, he used visitations, the periodic enquiries ordered by the archbishops, bishops and their subordinate archdeacons about what was going on each parish. The questions (articles of enquiry) were based on the Anglican canons, but each bishop interpreted the canons in his own way in a list of instructions, which (since the canons did not comprehensively lay down the law about every single aspect of church life) left a good deal of room for manoeuvre. The lay churchwardens of each parish (whose responsibilities were similar to those of the elders/churchwardens in the church in Strasburg in the 1530s – Block 2) were summoned by the archdeacon to answer the questions. On the face of it, these surveys seem to be rather limited, but they do provide us with a surprising amount of information about the activities of ordinary people.

EXERCISE

Turn now to Anthology Document 3.5, 'Episcopal visitation articles and returns, 1630s', and look at extract (a). This is an extract from the 122 questions asked in the visitation of the parishes in the diocese of Hereford in 1635.

1   Looking at the headings (numbered 1-9) what do you notice about the range of activity encompassed?

2   Looking at the content of some of the sections, what can you tell about the relationship between church and state?

3   How might we use a document such as this to learn more about parish life?

Spend about 20 minutes on this exercise.

1   These questions are not just about worship, or even about religious belief, they are about the behaviour and morality of everyone in the parish. There are special questions about medical practitioners, schoolmasters and midwives (who had to be licensed by the bishop).

2   The two are very closely connected. In point 1.1, parishioners are required to observe the king's declaration about settling religious differences, and in point 4, the clergy are required to 'teach and declare the lawful authority which the king hath over the state, both ecclesiastical and civil'. The idea of loyalty to the state was inextricably tied up with subscribing to a single ecclesiastical regime.

3   The headings and the questions themselves tell us what the authorities (the archbishops and bishops appointed by the king) considered to be important and what matters they considered to be disruptive of society. They cannot tell us about the king's subjects' private beliefs.

By comparing questions from visitations over a period of years, we can discover how the authorities' priorities changed. Thinking back to Block 2, you might expect, for example, that a visitation taking place during the reign of Henry VIII would ask different questions about church furnishings from those asked by a visitation in Elizabeth's reign. Compare the details of the placing of the communion table ('conveniently') in 1635 (Anthology Document 3.5(a), question 3.2) with Bishop Wren's orders of 1636 (Anthology Document 3.5(b)) in which parishes were instructed to place the table 'close under the wall of the chancel'. And in 1638, the visitation articles (Anthology Document 3.5(c)) contain a direct question about whether the altar is at the east end and railed off. But, as well as details of furnishings, the articles implicitly tell us something about the state and its ideology: its theory of rule. In Anthology Document 3.5(a), question 4, 'the just abolishing of all foreign power' is a reference to the widely held belief that Roman Catholics owed allegiance to the papacy (a foreign ruler) rather than to the king of England.

> **Matthew Wren** (1585–1667) was bishop of Hereford (1634), bishop of Norwich (1635) and bishop of Ely (1638–67). A close associate of Archbishop Laud, he was an enthusiastic exponent of his church reforms and was much hated by the numerous Puritans in his two East Anglian dioceses. He was held in the Tower of London for much of the Civil War and Interregnum and returned to his diocese at the Restoration.

To understand life in the parishes (and remember that most people lived in small rural settlements and not in towns) we need the *answers* to the questions provided by the churchwardens.

Turn again to Anthology Document 3.5, 'Episcopal visitation articles and returns, 1630s', and look at extract (d). The churchwardens of the parish of Shepreth were replying to the questions set out in Wren's visitation of 1638 (some of which are given extract (c) – the other questions were very similar to those in extracts (a) and (b)).

1   What offences were noted?

2   How compliant was the parish to the requirements?

Spend about 10 minutes on this exercise.

SPECIMEN ANSWER

1   One parishioner refused to pay the parish rate and another abused the minister.

2   The parishioners seem to have been most compliant and obedient to the requirements for baptism, marriage and taking Holy Communion, with an exemplary, politically loyal and conformist minister. The church had been rearranged with the communion table at the east end and steps up to it.

DISCUSSION

The performance of the parishioners seems almost too good to be true. Bishop Wren was subsequently charged with employing clerks to fabricate visitation returns for his diocese. However, very few actual returns survive. The matters that these questions dealt with might nowadays seem to be of little significance, but, as you will remember from Unit 4, the furnishings of a church carried important doctrinal messages, which the government used to display ecclesiastical changes in a manner evident to the meanest parishioner. The state actively used the beliefs of the church as a test of the loyalty of its subjects.

Personal rule or tyranny 1629–40?

What I hope you have seen from the first part of this section is how Charles I managed to alienate both his ordinary subjects and those whom we might call members of the political nation – MPs and peers, and the kinds of men (for they were only men) who were local government officers, such as justices of the peace, sheriffs and members of urban corporations. The issues that most antagonised them were his attempts to raise money in ways not authorised by parliament and to introduce religious changes that seemed to represent a return to a religious regime that was associated in many people's minds with tyranny. But, resistant though the population was to both Charles's financial expedients and the religious changes, he managed to govern perfectly satisfactorily on the income he had, especially after the country was extricated from foreign military enterprises in 1628.

Historians have long debated the significance of this period of royal government by prerogative, without parliament. Some take the view that this was a period of tyranny when Charles was fuelling fears about his absolutist political ambitions and his popish religious policies. Others take the view that Charles's policies, however unpopular, were not sufficient to cause a war. So what happened to turn a period of domestic peace into a civil war? Here we need to look beyond England.

Scotland, the prayer book and the bishops' wars

James VI had managed to make himself the most powerful king of Scotland since Robert the Bruce. He replaced the medieval idea of personal monarchy with the divine right of kings and bought the acquiescence of his more powerful subjects with grants of former church lands. James's accession to the English throne in 1603 did not diminish his power in Scotland, but Charles, succeeding to the throne in 1625, cared little for his northern kingdom and left its government to other bodies: the Privy Council in Edinburgh, comprising prominent laymen and lawyers and Scottish bishops (whose ecclesiastical powers were much less than those of English bishops); royal officials and judges; and the unicameral Scottish parliament (see Figure 10.2). Parliament met for the first time in Charles's reign when he visited the country in 1633 for his coronation. He had already, in 1625, ruffled feathers when, to improve church revenues, he had attempted to recover church lands granted to laymen, chiefly members of the Scottish nobility. In 1632, he commissioned a new building to provide a permanent home for the Scottish parliament and for the court of session (Figure 10.2). The following year (1633) he visited Scotland for his coronation and insisted that the English Book of Common Prayer be used instead of the Book of Common Order used in Scotland since the Reformation. He also asked the Scottish bishops to draw up a new liturgy based on that used in England.

Charles's desire, supported by Archbishop Laud, to impose greater religious uniformity between England and Scotland was prefigured in his father's attempts to give bishops in the Church of Scotland greater powers (there were no claims to apostolic succession as there were in England – bishops were seen as senior royal officials). The measure embodying this, the Five Articles of Perth (1618), required that the congregation receive the sacraments kneeling (we have already seen that this was a contentious matter in England), and was met with great opposition. A minister wrote in 1619 'every honest minister in all our east parts will rather leave their ministry or they yield one jot to the bishops' (Foster, 1975, p. 187). And the governing body of the Church of Scotland, the General Assembly of the Kirk, was given no opportunity to comment. In 1636, new church canons were published incorporating the Five Articles of Perth as well as elements of the English canons of 1604 and requiring the use of the liturgy still being composed by the Scottish bishops.

This new liturgy, published in 1637, was an amalgam of Scottish and English practice and was prefaced with a royal proclamation commanding its use. It provided for the communion table to be set altar-wise with its back to the east wall; the universal Scottish practice had been for communicants to sit on forms around the communion table and for communion to be administered no more than once a year after considerable preparation of fasting, sermons and examination of communicants. At its first major public airing, at St Giles Cathedral in Edinburgh on 23 July 1637, a riot broke out (see Figure 10.3). This was described by Henry Guthrie, a Church of Scotland minister:

> No sooner was the service begun, but a multitude of wives and serving women in the several churches, rose in a tumultuous way, and having prefaced awhile with despiteful [contemptuous] exclamations, threw the stools they sat on at the preachers and thereafter invaded them more nearly, and strove to pull them from their pulpits, whereby they had much ado to escape their hands, and retire to their houses. And for the bishop (against whom their wrath was most bent) the magistrates found difficulty enough to rescue him.
>
> (Fyfe, 1928, p. 137)

CVRIA Supremj Conventus Ordinum Regni Scotiæ
Vulgo Domus Parliamentj
The Parliament Houfe in Edinborrowgh by J.G.

F. de Wit excudit Amstelodami

THE PARLIAMENT HOUSE, EDINBURGH.

A reduced facsimile of a print engraved in Holland about the year 1640
from a drawing by the Revd James Gordon of Rothiemay.

Figure 10.2   James Gordon of Rothiemay/F. de Wit, *The Parliament House, Edinburgh* (designed by Sir James Murray of Killaherton), *c.* 1646, engraving. Photo: Reproduced courtesy of the Royal Commission on the Ancient and Historical Monuments of Scotland

More significant was the large number of petitions against the new liturgy and against 'the pride and avarice of the prelates seeking to overrule the whole kingdom' (Donaldson, 1978, p. 311). There followed a period of riots and disturbances in Edinburgh interspersed with royal proclamations against the petitioners, while the Scottish Privy Council tried to maintain order despite popular demands for the removal of bishops from the council. In November 1637, the petitioners elected their own delegates and forced the Privy Council to recognise them as a body with whom to negotiate.

JENNY GEDDES' STOOL.
(*From the Scottish Antiquarian Museum.*)

Figure 10.3   *Jenny Geddes' Stool*, St Giles, 1882, engraving, from James Grant, *Cassell's Old and New Edinburgh*, vol. 1 London, Cassell, Petter Galpin & Co., 1882, p. 146. Geddes, a poor market woman, allegedly initiated the stool throwing in St Giles's cathedral, but the first reference to her participation dates from 1670

> **Archibald Johnston of Wariston** (1611–1663) was lawyer, clerk of the General Assembly of 1638, a leading Covenanter and judge. He rejected the Engagement between the Scots and the king of 1647 and reluctantly accepted office during the Cromwellian occupation of Scotland in the 1650s. After the restoration of Charles II in 1660, he was sentenced to death and hanged for his part in the opposition to the king.

Meanwhile, Alexander Henderson and Archibald Johnston of Wariston, respectively a minister and lawyer, drew up a National Covenant, which stated that changes in the church required the approval of the General Assembly of the Kirk and parliament, and could not simply be decreed by the king; it said nothing about what innovations were acceptable. In February 1638, residents of Edinburgh signed it; it was then circulated to every burgh and parish for subscription and note was taken of anyone who refused to sign. In response, the king appointed the marquis of Hamilton to negotiate with the Covenanters but only to allow a General Assembly of the Kirk and a meeting of parliament if the Covenant was repudiated. By this time most nobles and lawyers had signed the Covenant and had already started to make military preparations. In September 1638, the king agreed to revoke the new prayer book and canons and to call a General Assembly in Glasgow in November 1638, the first to meet since 1618. The General Assembly pronounced on both the prayer book and the canons.

EXERCISE

Read Anthology Documents 3.6, 'The National Covenant, 1638', and 3.7, 'Acts of the General Assembly at Glasgow, 1638'. What differences do you notice between the two document extracts?

Spend about 15 minutes on this exercise.

SPECIMEN ANSWER

The extract from the Covenant is concerned with securing as wide agreement as possible that ecclesiastical innovations must be approved by 'free assemblies' and parliaments. Note the profession of obedience to religion and the desire not to diminish the king's authority. The General Assembly, by contrast, not only condemned the innovations and those who promulgated them ['pretended prelates' refers to the bishops; 'pretended' here means so-called rather than false], but threatened penalties against anyone using the new prayer book, so abhorrent were the doctrines it contained. It asserted the supreme jurisdiction of the General Assembly over any changes in the Church of Scotland and simply abolished bishops.

The radical steps taken by the General Assembly led to the marquis of Hamilton, the king's commissioner, trying to dissolve the meeting, but defiantly it sat on. Meanwhile, the Covenanters, who now included a number of aristocrats who had served in continental armies fighting the Thirty Years War, carried on arming. In March 1639, the king set forth for Scotland with an ill-equipped and poorly disciplined army, with the promise of troops to be sent from Ireland by Wentworth. Those Scots who had rallied to him (some of the Scottish nobility and many Highlanders, for example), rather than joining the Covenanters, had more success than the English forces, but not enough to prevent the English from being turned back at Berwick-on-Tweed by the Covenanting army under General Alexander Leslie. The agreement made at Berwick to end this First Bishops' War (more of a truce than a peace treaty since there had been no military engagement) required both sides to disband their armies while the king undertook to come to Scotland for meetings of parliament and the General Assembly of the Kirk.

Alexander Leslie (?1580–1661) had served with English forces in the Netherlands and as marshal in the Swedish forces in Germany. Returning to Scotland in August 1638, he led the Covenanting army in the First and Second Bishops' Wars, and the Scots army that joined the parliamentary forces in 1644. When the Scots declared for the king in 1647, Leslie (now Lord Leven) was relieved of his command. He reluctantly led a Scots army against Cromwell and was defeated at Dunbar (1650). He was held prisoner for a time in London, but was released and spent the rest of the Interregnum at home in Fife.

It soon became apparent that neither side was sincere. The Covenanters did not disband their army and Charles insisted on the inclusion of bishops in the forthcoming General Assembly. In August 1639, despite the fact that the king had returned to London, a new General Assembly met in Edinburgh, re-enacted the acts of the Glasgow Assembly and declared bishops not merely to be contrary to the laws of the church, but contrary to the law of God (a direct challenge to the king who appointed them). The parliament that met in Edinburgh later in the month confirmed the General Assembly's acts and, when the king ordered its prorogation, argued that it could not be prorogued without its own consent. It did, however, cease meeting and appointed representatives to carry on business until it should next meet.

The king was taken up with matters in England while the Covenanters mustered their forces and, in August 1640, the Scots army crossed the River Tweed and headed towards Newcastle. The English army was commanded by the earl of Northumberland, lord high admiral of England, a man with little naval expertise let alone the military experience of the Scots Thirty Years War veterans. Violent scenes took place between his mutinous troops and English civilians. The English forces were routed at Newburn, while citizens of nearby Newcastle (who had already displayed their opposition to the king's policies) welcomed the Scots army. Even the citizens of London greeted the Scots' victory with joy. The king's forces in Scotland proved unable to defend Edinburgh, and in October 1640 negotiations between king and Covenanters opened in Ripon, Yorkshire. The settlement they agreed required the king to pay the Scots army £850 a day as long as it remained on English soil, a sum which Charles certainly could not find from his ordinary revenues.

EXERCISE

Think now about these events in the light of our themes: state formation and beliefs and ideologies. I suggested in Unit 9 that Scotland could not claim to be a fully fledged state, but the actions of the Scots suggest that they regarded themselves as sovereign over such matters as the control of the church. Were ideas about the state driving religious changes or was religion the motive for demands about secular power?

Spend just a few minutes on this exercise.

It is very hard to say which came first. Charles felt entitled to govern the Scottish church without either the intervention of the ecclesiastical power (the General Assembly) or the secular power (the Scottish parliament). For many Scots, however, especially the most ardent supporters of the Covenant, the idea of the church being governed by a secular power was abhorrent (hence the declaration that bishops, appointed by the king, were against the law of God). For them, the proper government of the church was through the Presbyterian parish assemblies representing the sum of believers. But this was not a democratic ideology, it was a theocratic one.

Apart from the difficulty of disentangling religious and secular motivations, we might want to ask whether the First and Second Bishops' Wars could be construed as wars of self-determination. They were certainly inspired by a violent reaction against the imposition of English religious innovations. The Scots then limited the king's power by statute, placing him *under* the law. So the National Covenant is sometimes regarded as a nationalist declaration, for the movement it inspired was not solely religious.

The Short Parliament and the early months of the Long Parliament

We left Charles in England governing without parliament, with an income raised by a variety of contrivances and Archbishop Laud embarking on church reforms that roused popular opposition and encouraged sympathy for the Scots. But what impact did the Scots rebellion have on the fragile balance of Charles's relations with his English subjects? (We are retracing our steps to before the First Bishops' War, so look at the chronology in the *Course Guide* to see how these events fit together.)

The Scots mobilisation for the First Bishops' War, in the spring of 1639, required the king immediately to raise an army; with no money to pay it he was forced to conclude the pacification of Berwick. In the autumn of 1639, his close ally Thomas Wentworth returned to London from Dublin and, in anticipation of further trouble in Scotland, advised him to call the English parliament, which, Wentworth believed, could be managed to fund an effective campaign against the Scots.

MPs who met in April 1640 lost no time in reviewing the wrongs. As the earl of Clarendon (an MP in this parliament) wrote many years later:

> Mr Pym, a man of good reputation ... brake the ice; and, in a set discourse of above two hours, after mention of the King with the most profound reverence and commendation of his wisdom and justice, he observed that by the long intermission of Parliaments many unwarrantable things had been practised, notwithstanding the great virtue of his majesty: and then enumerated all the projects which had been set on foot, all the illegal proclamations which had been published and the proceedings which had been upon those

proclamations, the judgment upon ship-money, and many grievances
which related to the ecclesiastical jurisdiction; summing up shortly
and sharply all that most reflected upon the prudence and justice of
the government; concluding, that he had only laid that scheme before
them that they might see how much work they had to do to satisfy
their country.

(Clarendon, 1888, vol. 1, pp. 174–5)

John Pym (1584–1643) first sat as an MP in 1614 and emerged in the 1620s as
an opponent of the king. He was unofficial leader of the House of Commons in
the Short Parliament and remained a leading figure in the early years of the
Long Parliament. He was one of the five MPs the king attempted to arrest in
January 1642. After the outbreak of war he advocated outright military victory
for parliament and fostering the Scots alliance.

Charles required £100,000 a month to fund the army, but he received little
sympathy from parliament. The House of Commons wanted consideration of
its grievances and announced that 'Till the liberties of the House and kingdom
were cleared, they knew not whether they had anything to give or no' (quoted
in Woolrych, 2002, p. 136). While Wentworth (now earl of Strafford)
attempted to persuade the House of Lords to support the king, Lord Saye and
Sele argued strongly for the right of the House of Commons to initiate votes of
taxation. Strafford's strategy divided the Lords and sowed dissention between
the two houses.

The Commons also questioned the king's right to commission Convocation
(the governing body of the Church of England) to prepare new ecclesiastical
canons embodying the changes intended 'to expel irreverence and profaneness'
and to return the church 'unto the former splendour of uniformity, devotion
and holy order, the lustre whereof for some years bypast hath been much
obscured' (Bray, 1998, p. 556). In short, the canons were to do away with the
practices beloved of Puritans who wanted more preaching and less ceremony
and to make law the reforms that Archbishop Laud had started. Debates in
parliament established the strength of the opposition to the proposed reforms
and there were sympathetic exchanges between some MPs and the rebellious
Scots. A further royal demand for supply was followed by parliamentary
procrastination, so the king dissolved parliament after three weeks, without a
single measure being agreed.

Strafford advised Charles that a forced loan raised from the City of London
and improved collection of Ship Money would support a short, sharp war to
crush the Scots. The earl then uttered the fateful words 'You have an army in
Ireland you may employ here to reduce this kingdom', words which were
almost certainly intended to mean reducing Scotland but which were
understood by the king's opponents, to whom they were leaked, to mean his
English subjects.

As we have seen, war with the Scots recommenced in the summer of 1640 and it soon became obvious that there was insufficient money to pay an army. A peace settlement was concluded with the Scots at Ripon in October 1640, and a new parliament met in London in November. The elections caused considerable excitement. In many constituencies several candidates contested each seat (earlier in the century it was quite usual there to be only one candidate). The franchise consisted of men of property, a minority of the adult population (see Unit 9, p. 32 for the details). Throughout England and Wales, public petitions presented to parliamentary candidates alluded to the threat to true religion, the long intervals between parliaments, and infractions of the rule of law during the personal rule.

The new parliament awakened high hopes in England and Wales, while the Scots hoped to see the reforms they had pushed through the Edinburgh parliament replicated in Westminster. Thomas Knyvett, a Norfolk gentleman, wrote home from London that 'reformation goes on again as hot as toast' (quoted in Coward, 1994, p. 189). Members were intent upon dismantling the hated changes of the last eleven years and they turned first against the man regarded as the chief architect, the earl of Strafford, adopting the expedient formula that it was not the king but the 'evil counsels' of his ministers that were responsible for the assaults on ancient liberties. John Pym, who had opened the Short Parliament with a lengthy and measured account of grievances, four days into the new parliament, exclaimed '[There is] a design to alter the kingdom both in religion and government. This is the highest of treason' (Kenyon, 1986, p. 189).

In the packed months that followed, the judges who had ruled in favour of Ship Money were impeached, Archbishop Laud was imprisoned, and Strafford's trial began, the principal charges against him being that he had sowed discord between king and people, had erected 'arbitrary and tyrannical government' in the north of England and in Ireland, and provoked the Second Bishops' War (Kenyon, 1986, p. 178). The prosecution found it impossible to convince an overall majority of Commons or Lords that Strafford was guilty of treason. But news of a plot by the English army in the north of England to seize the Tower of London and release Strafford fortified parliament's resolve. Eventually the Commons passed an Act of Attainder asserting Strafford's guilt and sentencing him to death. Under the threat of violence, the king signed the Act, agreeing at the same time that parliament could not be dissolved without its own consent. He went on to sign: an Act abolishing the hated prerogative courts of High Commission and Star Chamber (which had been used to effect against his opponents); an Act against Ship Money; and a Triennial Act requiring a meeting of parliament for at least fifty days in every three-year period. Parliament discussed whether they should insist that royal counsellors be men in whom parliament had confidence (they stopped short of the Scots position under which the Scottish parliament could control the appointment of ministers).

At the same time, parliament condemned the newly issued English ecclesiastical canons and, in December 1640, a petition from London was presented to the House of Commons declaring that:

> whereas the government of archbishops and lord bishops, deans and archdeacons, etc., with their courts and ministrations in them, have proved prejudicial and very dangerous both to the Church and Commonwealth ... And whereas the said government is found by woeful experience to be a main cause and occasion of many foul evils ...

> We therefore most humbly pray and beseech this honourable assembly ... that the said government, with all its dependencies, roots and branches, may be abolished.

> (Kenyon, 1986, p. 154)

Several counties produced similar petitions and, in May 1641, a Bill to remove bishops 'root and branch' was moved in parliament. But by this time, it had become clear that MPs were deeply divided about how to settle the church, and counter-petitions in favour of bishops began to arrive. Strafford's trial had also split parliament and a party supporting the king had started to emerge. It was at this moment that news reached London of the outbreak of rebellion in Ireland.

EXERCISE

How would you characterise the development in parliament of opposition to the king?

Spend just a few minutes on this exercise.

SPECIMEN ANSWER

At the first meeting of the Short Parliament, MPs were unified by their demand for the redress of grievances, notably stopping the king from raising taxation without parliament's consent and reforming the church. But Strafford's policy of trying to divide parliament was successful, and by the time he was put on trial there was a considerable body of support for the king from MPs and lords who feared that matters were going too far. By the time the new parliament met, a party in support of the king, bishops and Strafford had started to emerge.

Ireland and 1641

Despite its proximity to England and the familiarity of Irish people to the English, Ireland was an object of almost anthropological curiosity. English rulers had, since Henry VIII declared himself king of Ireland in 1541, considered the place to be the haunt of barbarians. Rebellions by Gaelic lords in the late sixteenth century had established in many English minds that the Catholic Irish were not to be trusted. The government expropriated rebels' land and instituted schemes to grant it to Protestant English and Scots settlers (planters), extending the region of Protestant settlement from the area surrounding Dublin to King's and Queen's counties (Counties Laois and Offaly), parts of the province of Munster, and substantial tracts of Ulster.

Much of the writing about the country either expatiated on the quaintness of the Irish (in the hopes of encouraging English families to settle there) or on their lack of civility (providing authors with opportunities to describe Irish lasciviousness and the dirt in which they lived for the amusement of an English audience and justifying the seizure of land from rebel leaders). A characteristic description is that of Barnaby Rich.

EXERCISE

Read Anthology Document 3.8, 'The nature of the Irish, 1610 (Barnaby Rich)'. What impression does Rich convey of the Irish?

Spend about 15 minutes on this exercise.

SPECIMEN ANSWER

Rich starts by saying how similar the English, Scots and Irish were, and how superior to other races. But he quickly remarks on the uncivilised dress of the Irish from the remote parts and on the undesirable qualities of character which he attributed to their Catholicism or, rather, their adherence to the pope in preference to the government of the king of England.

As we saw in Unit 9 (p. 36), Ireland was a complex, multicultural society of Gaelic Irish, Old English, New English and Scots. In 1628, Charles I recognised the loyal protestations of the Old English by assuring them, in a document known as the Graces, of titles to land they had occupied undisputed for more than sixty years and by no longer requiring of heirs that they take the Oath of Supremacy, which was unacceptable to Catholics because it declared the monarch to be head of the Church of England/Ireland. It was agreed that, in return, the Irish parliament (which was traditionally dominated by the Old English) would grant the king revenue.

Charles I had little knowledge of Ireland. In 1633, he sent Thomas Wentworth to Dublin as lord deputy, knowing that Wentworth would wish to carry out the 'policy of thorough' to improve the administrative efficiency of the government and, more important, to increase tax revenues. Wentworth wanted also to reform the church and improve the position of Church of Ireland bishops, but his reference in a letter to his friend Archbishop Laud to 'reducing this kingdom to a conformity in religion with the church in England' reveals that this was not to be achieved by negotiation (Knowler, 1740, vol. 1, p. 187).

In 1634, Wentworth called a parliament in Dublin. The Old English members wanted to grant him subsidies in return for the ratification of the Graces; the New English, however, believed that a better way of raising money would be stricter enforcement of fines levied from Catholics for not attending Protestant Church of Ireland services. Wentworth's administrative reforms removed the financial attractions of holding office in the Dublin government (antagonising the New English), while his attempts to restore to the Church of Ireland church lands that had passed to the hands of laypeople, antagonised the Old English, especially when it became apparent that parliament would not ratify those sections of the Graces that guaranteed their land titles. He also alienated those of the New English who occupied former church lands.

Had it been obvious to the inhabitants of Ireland that Wentworth was incorruptible, he might have found some support, but he appeared to be taking advantage of his position to obtain for himself nearly 60,000 acres of land and to build a magnificent palace at Naas, some 20 miles outside Dublin. Subsequent investigation, however, proved that Wentworth's acquisitions were honestly obtained. Wentworth's particular crime, in the eyes of the inhabitants of Ireland, was to regard the country as a source of men and money to help the king out of his troubles in his other kingdoms.

In October 1641, unanticipated by the governments in either Dublin or London, the Catholic Irish in Ulster erupted in rebellion (see Figure 10.4). 'The uprising in Ulster was not the response to some specific English act or policy, but rather an outburst against immemorial grievances ... . [The conspirators'] motives were as vague as their plans' (Bottigheimer, 1971, pp. 30–1). Parliament in London prepared to ask the City of London for a loan of £50,000 to fund an army to be sent to Ireland.

Had the rising been confined to Ulster, matters would have been relatively straightforward, but in December 1641 the Old English (a group traditionally loyal to the crown, though largely Catholic) joined the rebels. The historian Nicholas Canny characterises the change as 'nothing short of a revolution', but one which was out of the control of the original leaders, who were unable to restrain the outburst of popular fury by native Irish against the Protestant settler communities of Ulster, Munster and Leinster (Canny, 1987, p. 208). The violence of the rising was branded on everyone's consciousnesses: estimates of the number of Protestants killed range from 4,000 (by historians) to 200,000 (by propagandists). Undoubtedly many more people died from famine and pestilence, and from the theft and destruction of livestock and crops.

This episode looms large in the consciousness of Ulster Protestants to this day and it is one whose history is difficult to write dispassionately, since virtually all the surviving testimony comes from Protestants' sworn depositions about the injury and loss they had suffered, often taken some years after the event.

EXERCISE

Read Anthology Document 3.9, 'Protestant depositions in Ireland, 1641', parts (a) and (b).

1   What can we tell about the deponents themselves?

2   Are these accounts likely to be accurate in all particulars?

Spend about 20 minutes on this exercise.

SPECIMEN ANSWER

1   We know that these deponents were women and were all unable to write their names (from which we may deduce that the accounts were written down by clerks). One deponent was the widow of an inn-keeper and evidently quite prosperous.

2   Both accounts contain a good deal of hearsay evidence and the similarities in
    the accounts, given that the women had not written them down themselves,
    might give rise to the suspicion that the clerks who recorded the depositions
    used stock phrases. But both accounts are extremely specific, naming Catholic
    rebels, people who were neighbours and known to the deponents, and providing
    details about places. Nevertheless, bearing in mind Rich's account of the Irish, it
    is difficult not to suspect some stereotyping of what the rebellious Irish were
    expected to do.

DISCUSSION

These depositions, despite their one-sided view of the events of 1641, are an
extremely important source for the history of the rising because there is so little
other material. Although they contain a great deal of hearsay evidence, they identify
by name many of the rebels, they provide some eye-witness accounts, and they tell
us about the mentality of the Protestant settlers, many of them people of humble
circumstances.

The spread of the rebellion beyond Ulster increased the urgency of defeating
the insurgents, and to do this the king had to have an army. In November 1641,
parliament at Westminster resolved to send 12,000 men from England and to
ask the Scots to send 10,000 more. Some troops arrived in Ireland in January
1642, and 2,500 Scots finally arrived in Ireland in April. It was not until
February that parliament in London passed, and the king signed, an Act for
Reducing Ireland under which individuals would advance money to suppress
the rebellion and in exchange be guaranteed lands in Ireland from those yet to
be confiscated from the undefeated rebels. Slowly, an army was gathered in
England under the command of Philip Lord Wharton, but in July 1642 his
officers were ordered by parliament to remain in England to serve against the
king and it was not until 1649 that a serious attempt was made from England
to defeat the Irish rebels.

Back to England

How was it that since the autumn of 1641 matters had deteriorated to such a
point that parliament required an army with which to confront the king?
Parliament had already shown itself susceptible to the idea of a popish
conspiracy, and the rising in Ireland fulfilled MPs' worst fears. In December
1641, despite the concessions already made by Charles, parliament presented
him with their Grand Remonstrance (passed by eleven votes) setting out their
demands (Anthology Document 3.10, 'The Grand Remonstrance, 1641',
provides an extract). The Grand Remonstrance listed those who were
considered responsible for 'subverting the fundamental laws and principles of
government': Jesuits and papists, bishops and the corrupt part of the clergy,
courtiers who had 'engaged themselves to foreign princes'. It called for a
synod of divines from England and other Protestant countries to advise on
settling the church, for the effective execution of the laws against papists and
for the king to appoint only such ministers as parliament might have
confidence in 'without which we cannot give his majesty such supplies for

At one Mr. Atkins house 7 Papistes brake in & beate out his braines, then riped upe his wife with Childe, after they had rauished her, & Nero like vewed natures bed of conception then tooke they the Childe & sacrificed it in the fire

English Protestantes striped naked & turned into the mountaines, in the frost, & snowe, whereof many hundreds are perished to death, & many lyinge dead in diches & Sauages upbraided them saynge now are ye wilde Irish as well as wee.

Figure 10.4   Illustrations from *The Teares of Ireland wherein is lively presented as in a map, a list of the unheard off cruelties and perfidious treacheries of bloud-thirsty Jesuits and the Popish faction*, London, A. N. for John Rothwell, 1642, p. 23. Photo: The British Library. This is one of the more luridly illustrated of the many accounts of the Catholic assaults on Protestants in the early months of the rising support of its own estate, nor such assistance to the Protestant party beyond the sea, as is desired' (Gardiner, 1906, pp. 202–32). Rioting in London and the gathering of soldiers to join Wharton's force for Ireland increased tension and Charles, in one of his most unwise moves, attempted in January 1642 to seize and impeach five MPs and one peer on the grounds that they (repeating the words of the Grand Remonstrance) had attempted to subvert the laws of the kingdom. Forewarned, the men had absented themselves from parliament. Meanwhile, parliament was working on a Bill to allow parliament to nominate the lords lieutenant (the royal official in each county responsible for levying the militia). Charles refused to sign the Bill and retreated to York. Parliament passed the Bill as an Ordinance (a law without royal assent) and nominated new lords lieutenant. Further negotiations took place, culminating in the Nineteen Propositions, in which parliament increased its demands beyond those of the Grand Remonstrance, calling on the king to place his children's upbringing and marriages in the hands of parliament. Shortly after, the king issued his own commissions of array to gentlemen in the shires, implicitly setting aside the Militia Ordinance and ordering the mustering of forces to create his own army.

TAKING SIDES

So far, we have looked at the events leading up to the outbreak of war and we might discern in them some of the causes of war. But we have already seen that finding a direct causal connection between one event and another is by no means straightforward. The king, by depriving his subjects of the usual means of challenging his actions through parliament, did a great deal to alienate them. But actually taking up arms, not just against your ruler, but also against your fellow citizens, is a far cry from objecting to unjust exactions. These were not just tax riots or popular demonstrations; this was a substantial part of the political nation, the people in whose hands the government of the country rested, mobilising an army against similar people.

What persuaded people to join one side or the other? Just as the English population at the time of the Wars of the Roses (Block 1, p. 110) found it difficult to take sides, so did the English population in 1642. The allegiances of men such as John Pym and John Hampden were not in doubt, nor were those closely connected with the royal court. The ironworkers of Birmingham, 'then a small town noted for its Puritanism and its ironwork', made up their minds quickly and supplied the earl of Essex, commander-in-chief of the parliament's forces, with 15,000 sword blades and imprisoned the messengers who brought royal orders to make weapons for the king (Gardiner, 1893, vol. 1, p. 107). But for the vast majority of people, the decision was not so straightforward. Conrad Russell makes the important point that confessional allegiance was not identical to political allegiance; that is to say, that not everyone who disapproved of the king's religious policies necessarily felt that it was legitimate to take up arms against the divinely ordained monarch, while not everyone who objected to the king's bending of the constitution revolted against his religious policies (Russell, 1990, p. 20). Many people took a long time to decide for one side or the other and it has become evident, through the excellent county histories that have been published for many English (though few Welsh or Scots) counties, that local politics could influence allegiances.

EXERCISE

Read Andy Wood, 'Beyond post-revisionism? The Civil War allegiances of the miners of the Derbyshire "Peak country"', *Historical Journal*, vol. 40, no. 1 (1997), pp. 23–40, which you looked at in the course introduction and can access through the course website. Concentrate on pp. 28–36. How does Wood characterise the miners' allegiance?

Spend about 30 minutes on this exercise.

SPECIMEN ANSWER

Wood suggests that the miners were politicised by challenges from landowners to their rights to work independently, but that religion (in particular Puritanism) had little impact on them (here Wood contrasts his view with those of other historians). On p. 32, Wood draws attention to the incentives offered by the king to miners and concludes (p. 35) that they were actually deeply divided between king and parliament.

CONCLUSION

The causes of the Civil War have been a subject for debate virtually since the war began. Rushworth and Nalson, extracts from whose histories you read in Unit 9, were writing about them in the seventeenth century. You will remember that both wrote their accounts, as they saw it, to set the record straight. And such differences continue to the present day.

EXERCISE

Reread Austin Woolrych, 'Shifting perspectives on the Great Rebellion', *History Today*, November 2002, no. 11, pp. 46–9 (which you printed out or downloaded for an exercise in Unit 9) and the set book, Wallace, pp. 138–9.

1   What different approaches to the causes of the Civil War does Woolrych describe? (Try to think of broader categories rather than the individual historians.)

2   What approach does Wallace adopt?

Spend about 20 minutes on this exercise.

SPECIMEN ANSWER

1   Woolrych describes three main approaches.
   (a)   Those derived from the interest of historians in whether different social classes were on the decline or the ascendant. For some historians, the primary interest has been in the economic dominance of one class or another. For others, it has been to do with the political influence to which different classes had access.
   (b)   The detailed, empirical studies of the personnel of English politics, whether in parliament, the royal administration or the city of London, on the one hand, or in local government in the counties, on the other.
   (c)   The studies of events in Scotland and Ireland that draw attention to the interconnectedness of developments in the three kingdoms.

2 Inevitably, Wallace emphasises the religious causes (though he mentions the constitutional discontents of the 1630s). He mentions differences between Protestants in England and Scotland, and the differences between Protestants and Catholics in Ireland.

DISCUSSION The debate that has taken place over the causes of the Civil Wars has been not so much between these different groups of historians as within them. You can see that the Marxist interpretation has influenced many historians who were or are not themselves Marxist. The studies of the personnel of English politics have led to strongly worded debates about the role of the House of Lords and its relationship with the House of Commons in the 1640s. County studies have drawn attention to the strength of the neutralist movements (those who said 'a plague on both your houses') and to the variety of local conditions and allegiances that might affect individuals' choices about which side to take (as we saw with Derbyshire). You saw, in Unit 9, something of the substance of 'the new British history', and earlier in this unit you have seen the way in which the Bishops' Wars and the Ulster Rising affected developments in England.

The Civil Wars began as a result of a series of complicated events driven by irreconcilable attitudes to religion and royal power. Opposition concentrated around the king's ideology of rule and the organisation and practices of the church. There seems to have been little disagreement about the existence of a monarchical state; even in 1642, no one expected much more than modest reforms. The idea of a revolution and the overthrow of the monarchy was far from their minds.

REFERENCES

Bottigheimer, K.S. (1971) *English Money and Irish Land*, Oxford, Oxford University Press.

Braddick, M. (1996) *The Nerves of State: Taxation and the Financing of the English State, 1558–1714*, Manchester, Manchester University Press.

Bray, G. (ed.) (1998) *The Anglican Canons 1529–1947*, Church of England Record Society, vol. 6, Woodbridge, Boydell Press.

Canny, N. (1987) *From Reformation to Restoration: Ireland, 1534–1660*, Dublin, Helicon Press.

Clarendon, Edward Hyde, earl of (1888) *The History of the Rebellion and Civil Wars in England*, ed. W. Dunn Macray, 6 vols, Oxford, Clarendon Press.

Coward, B. (1994) *The Stuart Age*, 2nd edn, Harlow, Longman.

Donaldson, G. (1978) *Scotland: James V – James VII*, Edinburgh History of Scotland, vol. 3, Edinburgh, Oliver and Boyd.

Foster, W.R. (1975) *The Church before the Covenants: The Church of Scotland 1596–1638*, Edinburgh, Scottish Academic Press.

Fyfe, J.G. (ed.) (1928) *Scottish Diaries and Memoirs 1550–1746*, Stirling, Eneas Mackay.

Gardiner, S.R. (1893) *History of the Great Civil War*, new edn, 4 vols, London, Longman Green.

Gardiner, S.R. (1906) *Constitutional Documents of the Puritan Revolution 1625–1660*, 3rd edn, Oxford, Clarendon Press.

Kenyon, J.P. (1986) *The Stuart Constitution 1603–1688: Documents and Commentary*, 2nd edn, Cambridge, Cambridge University Press.

Knowler, W. (ed) (1740) *The Earl of Strafford: Letters and Dispatches*, 2 vols, Dublin.

Laud, W. (1847–60) *The Works of the Most Reverend Father in God*, 9 vols, Oxford.

Russell, C. (1990) *The Causes of the English Civil War*, Oxford, Oxford University Press.

Sharpe, K. (1992) *The Personal Rule of Charles I*, New Haven and London, Yale University Press.

Stone, L. (1965) *The Crisis of the Aristocracy*, Oxford, Oxford University Press.

Stone, L. (1972) *Causes of the English Revolution*, London, Routledge and Kegan Paul.

Stone, L. (ed.) (1974) *The University in Society*, 2 vols, Princeton, Princeton University Press.

Stone, L. and Stone, J.F. (1984) *An Open Elite?*, Oxford, Oxford University Press.

Tawney, R.H. (1928) *English Constitutional Conflicts of the Seventeenth Century 1603–89*, Cambridge, Cambridge University Press.

Woolrych, A. (2002) *Britain in Revolution 1625–60*, Oxford, Oxford University Press.

Anne Laurence

INTRODUCTION

By far the most significant event of the war in England and its aftermath was the execution of the king on 30 January 1649. Despite the fact that many people were convinced that the only hope of peace was to be rid of a weak and duplicitous ruler, there was a terrible shock as the executioner's axe fell. At that moment, in the words of a witness to the scene, there went up 'such a groan as I never heard before, and desire that I may never hear again' (Wedgwood, 1971, p. 219).The archbishop of Armagh, James Ussher, saw the preliminaries of the execution from the roof of Lady Peterborough's house in St Martin's Lane, but fainted when 'the villains in vizards began to put up his hair' (*Dictionary of National Biography on CD-ROM*, 1988, 'Ussher').

But did Charles's execution have the same impact in his other two kingdoms? His heir, Prince Charles, was declared king in Scotland (parliament in England had hastily declared it illegal to proclaim anyone king after Charles I's execution) and was crowned a few months before the Scots were defeated decisively by the English at the battle of Worcester in 1651. In 1649, a substantial part of Ireland was under the control of the Catholic Confederation of Kilkenny, which had concluded a truce with the earl of Ormond and the royal forces he commanded there. Perhaps the most emblematic event of the period in Ireland was the capture of Drogheda by parliament's forces in 1649 and the massacre there – the prelude to the victory of parliament over both the Catholic rebels and the royalist forces in Ireland.

We cannot hope to cover all the ins and outs of the wars and their aftermath in the length of this unit, so I shall concentrate on those aspects of the wars that relate most closely to the themes of the course. We shall also see rather more of events in England than in Scotland and Ireland. While the general subject of the unit is how the Wars of the Three Kingdoms led to the execution of the king and its consequences for the three kingdoms, culminating in 1660 with the restoration of the monarchy, we shall concentrate on:

- how the divisions between the combatants were dictated by their beliefs and ideologies
- how warfare affected producers and consumers
- whether the nature of the state altered in the 1650s.

As well as thinking about the Wars of the Three Kingdoms, you will work on a selection of documents and learn to use the online *Oxford Dictionary of National Biography*.

BELIEFS AND IDEOLOGIES IN THE WARS 1642–49

The historian Conrad Russell noted that whatever the longer term causes of conflict might have been, it was the failure of the political process that forced the taking up of arms in England in 1642, for many of the subjects about which the two sides disagreed had divided them for a long time (Russell, 1990, p. 19). We might also argue that it was the failure of the political process in Scotland and Ireland that led to Scots and Irish taking up arms against the English in 1638 and 1641, respectively. Certainly the difficulties of balancing the claims of three kingdoms, each with a distinctive religious character, with his own convictions about the nature of kingship and the church, placed demands on Charles that he was ill placed to meet. Having got to the point of war, however, some kind of conviction kept men fighting, and in this section we shall look at the beliefs and ideologies that divided the parties.

Taking sides: England 1642–43

We left the king in June 1642, having issued instructions to the lords lieutenant in each English and Welsh county to raise troops under their own commissions of array and to ignore parliament's Militia Ordinance. We can get a sense of the relative strength of feeling for each side by looking at where the measures were implemented.

EXERCISE

Look at the *Visual Sources*, Plates 11.1 and 11.2.

1   What do you notice about the strength of support for the parliament's Militia Ordinance?

2   What do you notice about the strength of support for the king's Commissions of Array?

Spend about 15 minutes on this exercise.

SPECIMEN ANSWER

1   The Militia Ordinance was implemented in fourteen counties between May and July and a further nine between August and October, out of a possible forty counties in England. The counties were predominantly in the east and south of England. It was not implemented in any of the twelve Welsh counties.

2   Commissions of Array were executed in ten English counties, predominantly in the north and west of the country, and one Welsh county. Commissions failed in a further twelve counties, predominantly in the Midlands.

DISCUSSION

From this one would deduce that there was stronger support for parliament than for the king. However, the four most northerly counties followed neither set of instructions, nor did Dorset, Derbyshire, Huntingdonshire or most of Wales. In five counties, both the Militia Ordinance and the commission of array were fully executed, and in a further six counties attempts were made to execute both. We should not assume that in those counties where neither measure was implemented the population was simply indifferent; the Staffordshire gentry were determined to remain neutral. The maps show that the population of England and Wales was not clearly divided between king and parliament and they hint at, but do not allow us accurately to predict, the geography of allegiance that was to emerge by the mid-

1640s. This reinforces the points made in the article 'Beyond post-revisionism?' by Andy Wood (which you read in Unit 10) about the complexity of the reasons for people's allegiance.

For those who were actively involved as MPs, or who had to respond either to parliament's Militia Ordinance or to the king's Commission of Array, or who had particularly strong religious convictions, the war started in August 1642. Two-thirds of peers joined the king, but a majority of the House of Commons supported parliament. Both peers and MPs raised troops for the army. For the vast majority of other people, the war started a good deal later, as the leading historian of localism in the Civil Wars has written, 'Less than one third of the supporters of each side actually took up a military or civilian position in the years 1643–5 ... The bulk of the gentry were reluctantly involved in the conflict' (Morrill, 1974, pp. 73, 74). And, of the moderates, he said, 'the hallmark of the moderate was that he wanted to obey *both* sides, not *neither*, and when one side issued a direct and personal order he acquiesced. Those not directly charged by either side could and did continue to sit on the fence' (Morrill, 1976, p. 42). Many participants were as much preoccupied with local divisions as with events taking place in London or the king's headquarters at Oxford.

Nonetheless, much of England did mobilise, many thousands of people did go to war and many died as a result. Why was it that they felt so passionately that they were prepared to risk their lives? It is apparent that many people saw the king's religious innovations as connected with his infringement of their ancient rights. And the religious aspect of the armies began to be evident from the early months of the war.

Having raised their armies, the forces of king and parliament took to the field. Their first major engagement, on 23 October 1642, was at Edgehill, Warwickshire, a county that was to be much fought over in the coming years. The result was inconclusive, but in one respect it set the tone for the rest of the war. The king's forces were commanded by his nephew Prince Rupert. They chased parliament's cavalry off the field, but instead of turning on the now unprotected infantry, set about plundering the district. Parliament's army (under the command of Robert Devereux, 3rd earl of Essex (1591–1646)) was addressed before the battle by chaplains who rode among the soldiers 'through the thickest dangers, and in much personal hazard, most faithfully and courageously exhorting and encouraging the soldiers to fight valiantly, and not to fly' (Vicars, 1644, p. 200).

Prince Rupert (1619–1682), third son of the elector Palatine and nephew of Charles I, received his military training in Germany in the 1630s. He arrived in England in July 1642, was made general of the king's horse and, in 1644, commander-in-chief of the king's army. Court-martialled after the loss of Bristol, he was restored to favour but left England after the fall of Oxford and joined the French service. In 1649, he commanded a naval expedition to Ireland and privateering expeditions across the Atlantic and elsewhere. He joined Charles II in exile and returned to England in 1660, when he served Charles in various capacities.

The king's forces were not universally rapacious and irreligious, any more than parliament's forces were universally sober and godly. A Cambridgeshire gentleman, raising a force for parliament's East Anglian army in 1643, described what he was looking for:

> a few honest men are better than numbers ... If you choose godly honest men to be captains of horse, honest men will follow them ... I had rather have a plain russet-coated captain that knows what he fights for, and loves what he knows, than that which you call a gentleman and is nothing else.
>
> (Abbott, 1937, vol. 1, p. 256)

At the time that he wrote this, Oliver Cromwell was commander of a small force within the army of the Eastern Association, raised from the combined East Anglian counties and commanded by the earl of Manchester, an army subsidiary to the main forces under the earl of Essex.

Oliver Cromwell (1599–1658) was an East Anglian gentleman and MP. In 1642, he joined Essex's army as captain of horse but transferred to the army of the Eastern Association, rising to become second in command to the earl of Manchester. When the New Model Army was formed in 1645, he was appointed lieutenant-general to Fairfax, which he remained until 1649. He was appointed lord lieutenant of Ireland and commander-in-chief of the expeditionary force there in 1649, but was recalled by parliament to lead the expedition to Scotland in 1650. He dissolved the Rump Parliament in 1653. Barebone's Parliament surrendered their powers to him as commander-in-chief of the army and officers drew up a constitution appointing Cromwell protector. In 1657, he was offered and declined the crown, but he did agree to nominate a successor – his son Richard.

Propaganda, news and the press

In 1640, the censorship of the press that had been strictly enforced (by bishops and the Company of Stationers) lapsed. There was a sudden explosion of print materials, especially weekly or bi-weekly newsbooks that reported the progress of the war, and which increasingly represented the views of different factions within the two main sides.

Read Anthology Document 3.11, 'Newsbook accounts of an engagement at Warrington, 8 April 1643', extract (a) '*Mercurius Aulicus* (Royalist newsbook)'. In the Introduction to the course we provide you with a set of questions to use in looking at primary sources. To remind you of these, the exercise here follows them.

1   What kind of document is it?
    (a)   Who wrote it?
    (b)   Who was the intended audience/why was it written?
    (c)   When was it written?
    (d)   What type of document (public, private, official, published, etc.) is it?

2   What is its historical context? (You might want to look at the chronology in the *Course Guide*.)

3   Are there comments you can make on specific points in the text?

4   What is its significance for the study of our period?

Spend about 20 minutes on this exercise.

1   It is a newsbook (newspaper).
    (a)   The author was presumably editor or publisher of the newsbook.
    (b)   The intended audience, the readership of the newsbook, was anyone who could afford to buy it.
    (c)   On or after 9 April 1643.
    (d)   It is a public document, published and sold; it is one issue of series.

2   It provides an account of a military engagement in Cheshire between royalist and parliamentarian forces at a fairly early stage of the Civil Wars.

3   It was intended to celebrate the earl of Derby's victory, gained by a rather underhand subterfuge, and the defeat of the parliamentary forces under Brereton.

4   Even though this is a very small extract, we can deduce from its highly partisan account of the engagement that this was probably a royalist newsbook. So an important general point to make is that this was a war in which printed propaganda featured significantly.

We cannot assume that the readership was royalist because, though this particular newsbook was published in Oxford (the king's headquarters), there was a lively market in newsbooks and *Mercurius Aulicus* could also be obtained in London.

It is unlikely that the authors of the newsbook accounts were correspondents on the battlefields sending back reports to their editors in Oxford or London. It is much more likely that the newsbooks used official reports of the war and letters from the generals carried by scouts to London and Oxford. You can see, in Anthology Document 3.11, extract (b) '*The Kingdomes Weekly Intelligencer* (Parliamentarian newsbook)' and extract (c) '*A Continuation of certaine Speciall and Remarkable Passages from both Houses of Parliament*', corresponding accounts of the same episode from the parliamentary press. In considering the passage's significance for the study of our period, I have not focused on the specific information about the engagement in Cheshire. Information about what happened where is normally a matter of public record, but what we are concerned with here is the way in which this document was used for propaganda.

We might want to note the different use of the word 'perfected'. (You can always check on the meaning of obscure words by looking them up in the *Oxford English Dictionary* online, though the Open University online library. It is particularly valuable for looking up ancient meanings.)

The outpouring of publications was not restricted to newsbooks. Pamphlets on religious and political subjects, and satirical and polemical ballads and tracts poured off the presses. Illustrations played an important part in the more popular works, though it is questionable how far they were intended for an illiterate population because the pictures often contained text (see Figures 11.1 and 11.2). Particular subjects for illustration were atrocities (see Figure 10.4) and portraits of victorious generals.

Divisions among the parliamentarians 1642–48

The press was used not only to put out propaganda on behalf of the main protagonists in the conflict in England, but also in connection with the growing divisions among the supporters of parliament. For the most part, the king's supporters had an overwhelming sense that to rebel against the king was not simply treason, it was an offence against God. A good many of his supporters had opposed the religious innovations in the 1630s, but felt unable to take up arms against a king who held his powers from God, and there was a steady trickle of defections from parliament to the king among peers and MPs, many of them during 1643, the year of parliament's greatest military failure.

From the outset of the war, the parliamentary cause was far more of a coalition of competing interests than was the king's. The motives of parliament's supporters were more complicated and various than the loyalty to kingly rule that animated most royalists. For some people, the king's crimes against his subjects were offences against their ancient liberties as 'freeborn Englishmen'. They associated the king with economic changes that had worked to their detriment, such as the reduction in the amount of common land, the imposition of oppressive taxes and a lack of regard for freedoms that were guaranteed by the Magna Carta. For others, he had offended against their idea of rightly reformed Protestant religion by pressing forward with Laudian innovations.

Parliament's military failures of 1643 prompted them to seek an alliance with the Scots, who themselves wanted to guarantee the religious changes for which they had fought the Bishops' Wars. The treaty with the Scots, the Solemn League and Covenant, was ratified by parliament in September 1643. Pressure to conclude it came from events in Ireland, where soldiers became available to join the royal army in England by a cessation of arms between the king's Irish forces and the Catholic rebels. There were two parts to the Scots' treaty: a military alliance under which the Scots provided a substantial army to serve

Figure 11.1 Josiah Ricraft. *A perfect List of all the Victories obtained (through the blessing of God) by the Parliaments Forces*, London, 1646. Photo: The British Library. London printers produced broadsheets listing victories and extolling the virtues of the parliamentarian generals

Figure 11.2 *Victories Obtained (by Gods blessing on the Parliaments forces) both by Land and Sea*, London, 1647. Photo: the British Library. Woodcuts were extensively reused from one publication to another. Note how Alexander Leslie is reproduced in the two broadsheets.

Figure 11.2 (detail)

and be paid for by parliament, and an agreement about the future of religion in England and Ireland.

EXERCISE

Now read Anthology Document 3.12, 'Religious provisions of the Solemn League and Covenant, September 1643' (see also Figure 11.3). What were the implications of the Solemn League and Covenant for the future of religion in England?

Spend about 10 minutes on this exercise.

SPECIMEN ANSWER

The English agreed to defend the reforms of the Church of Scotland implemented after 1639 (no bishops, no Book of Common Prayer) and to preserve reformed religion in England and Ireland. The definition of reformed religion 'according to the Word of God and the example of the best reformed churches in Europe' might seem to have offered scope for flexibility, but the requirement to bring the three churches 'to the nearest conjunction and uniformity' leaves little doubt that the English were signing up to implement a church settlement based on that of Scotland, especially after bishops and the other officers of the Anglican Church had been 'extirpated'.

The religious terms of the Scots alliance caused divisions among parliamentarians, which became more severe and more bitter as the years passed. The theocratic nature of the proposed ecclesiastical administration (giving overall responsibility to a general assembly of the church rather than parliament) was unpopular among many MPs and supporters of parliament. Attempts in 1643 and 1644 to ensure that all MPs, office holders and everyone with a military command had signed the Solemn League and Covenant met with some resistance.

We might view this division as a religious one, but it had political consequences, which we shall look at shortly. Another division that became apparent in 1644 was that between what we might call the victory party (who wanted to defeat the king decisively) and those who wished from an early stage to pursue peace (often people who had been close to the court before the war but who wanted to signal their opposition to the king's policies).

Following the spectacular parliamentary victory at the battle of Marston Moor (2 July 1644), for which the Eastern Association army under the command of the earl of Manchester was largely responsible, the earl seemed to lose faith in the need to win the war decisively. Oliver Cromwell, his lieutenant-general and an MP, increasingly bitter at the earl's failures, charged Manchester in the House of Commons with 'unwillingness ... to have this war prosecuted unto a full victory' (Abbott, 1938, vol. 1, p. 302). The divided command of an important part of parliament's military strength, the public row, and the antagonism between the two houses of parliament when Manchester invoked support from his fellow peers, did much to accelerate a measure that was to have far-reaching consequences – the Self-Denying Ordinance (which excluded from a seat in either house any soldier or office holder). This ideological division continued to affect the way in which parliament negotiated with the king and meant that there was a constant tension between those who

Figure 11.3 From *A Solemne League and Covenant for the Reformation and Defence of Religion, the honour and happinesse of the king, and the peace and safety of the three kingdoms of Eagland, Scotland, and Ireland*, Edinburgh, Printed by Evan Tyler, 1643, p. 5. Photo: Huntington Library, California. Page showing left, the ungodly and, right, the godly.

wanted to end the war quickly, even though it meant accepting that the king retained a number of significant powers, and those who wanted to pursue the war to exact the maximum number of concessions from the king. It is important to remember, however, that it was not until late in 1648 that anyone really thought of doing without a king altogether.

A further difference between the two men was Manchester's support for the work of the Westminster Assembly of Divines and Cromwell's opposition to it. Those who wanted a church settlement as proposed by the Assembly to reform the Church of England to bring it into conformity with Scotland's were known as Presbyterians. Their opponents (known as Independents) wanted a more devolved form of church organisation in which each congregation was paramount and which had no formal hierarchy of officers (such as bishops) or coercive powers (such as those exercised by the church courts). This difference emerged clearly in parliament, where Presbyterians (generally in favour of the Scots alliance) and Independents (generally opposed to it) began to act as separate interest groups. The Presbyterians formed a more cohesive group, more nearly resembling a modern political party, while the Independents were a looser alliance consistent with the kind of religious organisation they favoured.

Independents represented the emergence of a new kind of religious expression based on a multiplicity of individual congregations with an array of different religious beliefs. Laypeople gathered round them communities of like-minded believers who tried out new forms of preaching and different kinds of belief unrestricted by the rules of the Church of England and the discipline and academic theology of the Anglican clergy. Increasingly, for such people a return to royal government, with all its associations of an established church with legal enforcement of practices and beliefs, was unthinkable. Although few people were prepared to admit that what they wanted was religious toleration, that was the effect.

> **Thomas Fairfax** (1612–1671), a Yorkshire gentleman, served in the army of Sir Horace Vere in the 1620s. In 1642, he was appointed second in command of parliament's Northern Army, commanded by his father. In 1645, he was appointed by parliament commander-in-chief of the New Model Army, in which post he continued until 1650, when he resigned rather than invade Scotland. He lived quietly during the 1650s and was active in the moves to restore the king. He returned to private life after 1660.

Two developments promoted the spread of this religious heterodoxy. The first, as I have suggested, was the lapsing of censorship of the press and pulpit. The second was the creation of the New Model Army in April 1645. This was formed out of several of the existing forces to provide parliament with a much more effective fighting force than it had hitherto had. It differed from the earlier armies in that its officers, though largely gentry and richer tradespeople, no longer included peers and MPs (with the exception of Oliver Cromwell).

The absence of censorship encouraged the emergence of radical Protestants, who had worshipped in secret in the 1630s or who had gone into exile. At the same time, there was a groundswell of support for these new religious forms, especially in the cities and in the New Model Army. Although the army was provided with chaplains – a mixture of Presbyterians and Independents – the feature that most commentators remarked on was the large number of laymen who preached and established religious meetings within their own regiments. These laymen were influenced by Independents outside the army, and embraced a wide range of beliefs, some of which were regarded as heresy by orthodox Anglicans and Presbyterians. Figure 11.4 caricatures some of the more extreme beliefs – note the Anabaptist baptising someone by total immersion, the Libertine smashing the Ten Commandments, the naked Adamite and the Arminian (for Calvinist predestination had its radical as well as its Anglican critics).

In June 1645, 'the Royalist cause committed suicide' at the battle of Naseby (quoted in Woolrych, 2002, p. 316). Not only was this a crushing defeat, but letters captured from the king's baggage train made public Charles's negotiations with the Irish rebels. The victorious Cromwell, lieutenant-general to Fairfax, wrote to the speaker of the House of Commons saying:

> Honest men served you faithfully in this action, Sir, they are trusty; I beseech you in the name of God not to discourage them. ... He that ventures his life for the liberty of his country, I wish he trust God for the liberty of his conscience, and you for the liberty he fights for.
>
> (Quoted in Woolrych, 2002, p. 319)

His words reflect the growing distance between the army commanders and their civilian masters in parliament. Members of the army, mindful of the continued influence of the Scots, were concerned that parliament would negotiate a settlement with the king that would not justify to soldiers in the army the hardships they had undergone in the war.

In May 1646, following a series of military defeats by parliament, the king surrendered to the Scots army at Newark; in June, Oxford, headquarters of the royalist government, fell to parliament, and in July, negotiations for peace opened in Newcastle. While there was little chance that Charles would agree to swear the Solemn League and Covenant, the terms put to the king formed the basis for discussions for months to come. People were sick of the war with high taxation, free quarter and the depredations of passing armies, and disruption of normal life. The New Model Army's discipline more or less held, but mutinies broke out in many of the provincial forces.

Meanwhile, parliament debated what to do with its armies. By now, most soldiers were owed considerable arrears of pay, but parliament decided in October 1646 to keep the New Model Army intact for another six months because it was known that the king was looking for armed assistance from

Figure 11.4   *A Catalogue of the severall Sects and Opinions in England and other Nations, With a briefe Rehearsall of their false and dangerous Tenents*, London, printed by R.A., 1647. Photo: The British Library. Not all those pictured were heroes. The same lapsing of censorship that gave rise to a flourishing press also allowed freedom of religious expression. Many more conservative parliamentarians, especially those who were Presbyterian in religion, were horrified by the growth of what they regarded as heretical sects who took religious reform a step too far from the Anglican Church. Heresiographers (recorders of heresy) such as Thomas Edwards and Ephraim Pagitt sought to identify the enemy within. This broadsheet is loosely based on a longer work by Pagitt

Figure 11.4 (detail)

abroad. Lands confiscated from the English bishops were used to raise £200,000 to pay off and send home the Scots army in February 1647. In return, the Scots handed over the king to parliament, who lodged him at Holdenby or Holmby House, Northants.

At the same time, parliament determined to try to solve the problem of Ireland, where the fighting had continued spasmodically since 1641, and to pay off as much of the army as possible. Exaggerated claims made about the radicalism of the New Model Army and pressure from the generally Presbyterian City of London (responsible for raising such funds as parliament could not find from taxation) persuaded parliament to send New Model Army soldiers to Ireland and to keep on foot in England provincial forces more sympathetic to Presbyterianism. When this plan became known, petitions began to circulate within the army expressing the troops' concern about the payment of arrears, provision for indemnity against prosecution for acts committed in war, and their conditions of service in Ireland, especially given the uncertainty about who was to command the expedition. Delegates from parliament met an army council of forty-four New Model Army commanders in March; not one of the officers was prepared to serve in Ireland without satisfaction for their concerns. Petitioning continued in the army with soldiers, quite reasonably, repeating their demands, but parliament demanded that General Fairfax order them to stop and, in a panic, ordered the immediate disbanding of all forces except those destined for Ireland, while asserting that: 'all those who shall continue in their distempered condition, and go on advancing and promoting that petition, shall be looked upon and proceeded against as enemies of the State and disturbers of the public peace' (quoted in Gardiner, 1893, vol.3, p. 229).

From restricting their demands to military matters, the soldiers moved on to political reform. This alteration in their temper, like the growth of religious radicalism, was influenced by developments outside the army, especially in London. A number of Londoners known as Levellers, mostly lesser gentry and tradesmen, some of whom had served in the army, began to articulate demands that there should be religious toleration, that supreme power should rest with the Commons, that all oaths and covenants (including the Solemn League and Covenant) be repealed and that the law be reformed. Their leaders, John Lilburne, William Walwyn and John Wildman, had published many pamphlets and began to form close links with the army petitioners.

In April 1647, cavalry regiments in the New Model Army elected representatives or 'agitators' (in the seventeenth century, the word agitator did not have the modern connotation of stirring up, the meaning was more akin to 'agent') and in May the infantry regiments did likewise. The two agents for each regiment felt able to make representations independently of the senior command of the army and made efforts not only to articulate their military grievances but to express views about the postwar world. In June, the army seized the king from Holmby House, transferring power from parliament to the army though, as Fairfax was at pains to assure parliament, they sought 'no alteration of the civil government' (quoted in Woolrych, 2002, p. 371). A general council of the army, consisting of over 100 officers and agitators from most regiments in the New Model Army, met at Reading in July to discuss a comprehensive scheme for settling the government of the kingdom that was presented to the gathering by Cromwell's son-in-law, Commissary-General Henry Ireton, and known as the *Heads of the Proposals*. It was intended that these should form the basis for negotiations with the king. Following a falling out with parliament and the City of London, Fairfax transferred the army headquarters to Putney, on the outskirts of the city. Here, debates about the *Heads of the Proposals* continued while the rank and file of the army, increasingly influenced by the Levellers, asserted that their commanders were acting against them rather than for them. A new statement of soldiers' demands, *An Agreement of the People*, was presented and debated at Putney by officers, agitators and civilian Levellers.

EXERCISE

Read Anthology Document 3.13, 'Agitators and Levellers, 1647', part (a), 'An agreement of the people', and answer the following questions:

1   On whose behalf is the document presented?

2   By what right do the authors claim authority for the army to act?

3   What implications do the proposals have for the organisation of the state? (Think back to Table 9.1 in Unit 9.)

Spend about 10 minutes on this exercise.

SPECIMEN ANSWER

1   It is presented by the agents of the five regiments of horse and then 'by the general approbation of the army'.

2   The authors use the device of saying that God, by delivering victory to them, has justified their initiative; they also claim that, because of the lack of 'frequent national meetings in council' (by which they mean parliament) and their ineffectualness, the former oppressions have not been removed.

3   Parliamentary constituencies would be reorganised to ensure a more equal distribution of population between each one. The electorate was the supreme power. An elected parliament alone had the power to legislate, to appoint judges, JPs and other officers of the judiciary and executive, to make war and peace, and to conduct foreign policy. All of this would have meant removing powers from the king and the House of Lords. There was to be no established church with coercive powers, no conscription (both sides in the war had conscripted soldiers from 1643), and no postwar prosecutions.

DISCUSSION

Although no one had proposed abolishing the monarchy, what was proposed was a state whose head had no legislative, judicial or executive power. It was also a state which, with religious toleration, had no religious justification for the right of the rulers to rule. Instead, the consent of the electorate was taken to provide that justification.

EXERCISE

Read Anthology Document 3.13, 'Agitators and Levellers, 1647', extract (b), 'Extracts from the debates at Putney'. These extracts are not part of a continuous exchange between the participants but are representative of the views of the different groups. Answer the following questions:

1   What differences are there between Wildman and Ireton's views?

2   How does Rainsborough characterise the views of the rank and file soldiery?

Spend about 10 minutes on this exercise.

SPECIMEN ANSWER

1   Wildman appears to be arguing for a universal franchise on the basis of the free consent of the people, while Ireton (representing the senior officers of the army) appears to want a property qualification for electors, by which he means land rather than money.

2   Rainsborough asserts that the soldiers fought from conviction for their cause and that to insist on a property qualification for electors was to deceive the troops about the cause for which they had been fighting.

It is extraordinary that in five years, rank and file soldiers who, at the beginning of the war were starting to question the religious monopoly of the Church of England, were demanding constitutional reforms which implied what we would describe as a democratic republic. However, we need to beware of attributing too many modern thoughts to them. They did not envisage including women in the franchise and historians have discussed extensively whether they intended to allow servants to vote. Both women and servants were considered to be dependent on men (husbands, fathers, employers) who would represent the interests of their dependants. Leveller agitation in the army led to considerable discontent and to a widening breach between senior officers and soldiers, resulting in a number of courts martial for mutiny.

But while the army was debating the future, the king had escaped from the army's custody and was negotiating with the Scots. In December 1647, he concluded an Engagement with them under which he agreed to a limited implementation in England of the terms of the Solemn League and Covenant (see Anthology Document 3.14, 'Charles I's Engagement with the Scots'). In February 1648, the document became public, and war broke out in the spring with the Scots' occupation of Berwick and Carlisle and a rising in South Wales. A Scots army marched into England but was decisively defeated by the New Model Army at Preston in August. The Second Civil War, as this war was known, was a messy and violent affair and was accompanied by a rising in Scotland by extreme Covenanters who would have nothing to do with an uncovenanted king but who could not make common cause with the parliament's army, which they saw as filled with heretics. The king's Engagement with moderate Covenanters precipitated a split in Scotland that was to endure for decades to come.

Negotiations between parliamentary commissioners and the king opened at Newport on the Isle of Wight. The king made considerable concessions and agreement might conceivably have been reached with parliament but for the army, who believed that parliament was proposing to accept terms that would betray them. They removed the king from the Isle of Wight and marched on London. On 5 December 1648, parliament voted to continue to negotiate with the king and the following day a military force led by Colonel Pride ejected those members (many of them Presbyterians) who had supported the vote. The remaining MPs, known as the Rump, voted to bring the king to trial before a specially constituted High Court of Justice on the capital charges of committing treason and levying war against his people.

Scotland and Ireland

For the Scots, the primary goal was to assure the preservation of a rightly reformed church; this justified alliances with whomsoever would best guarantee that. There had, since 1643, been a Scottish royalist army led by the charismatic general Montrose. Montrose's defeat at Philiphaugh in 1645 led to the disbanding of the Scottish royalist forces in 1646. Meanwhile, the main Covenanting army served in England until paid off and sent home in 1647. Equally important had been the Scots commissioners in London, who worked with parliament and the Westminster Assembly of Divines to implement the terms of the Solemn League and Covenant. Their actions were directed from Scotland by the Scottish parliament (or, when it was not sitting, by the Committee of Estates) and by the General Assembly of the Kirk, whose primary interest was in securing a uniform religious settlement in a federalist polity. This agenda dominated Scots policy while being regarded as peripheral in England, for whom the alliance was much more one of 'political pragmatism and military expediency' (Macinnes, 1990, pp. 123–4).

Following the First Civil War, public offices in Scotland were purged of anyone tainted with royalism or who supported episcopacy; the Engagement brought back more moderate Covenanters (now known as Resolutioners) but the triumph of the radical Covenanters (now known as Protestors) was confirmed by their passing on 23 January 1649 the Act of Classes. This gave the church a veto over office holders and ensured that anyone who had anything to do with the Engagement with Charles I was excluded from any position of power.

Following the outbreak of the rising in 1641, the Gaelic Irish rebels, arguing that they were fighting *for* the king, secured the support of a significant number of influential Old English, creating a single Catholic bloc. In October 1642, the Catholic alliance set up a provisional government in Kilkenny, which proclaimed its support for God, king and country, and in which Catholic clergy were an important presence. In 1643, a papal nuncio joined the confederation; the second of these, Giovanni Battista Rinuccini, who arrived in 1645, proved a formidable leader and counterweight to the Catholic noblemen who saw themselves as the leaders of the Confederation. Freedom of worship for Catholics in the areas controlled by the Confederation exposed Irish Catholics to continental Catholic influences, especially those of the Council of Trent, which had set about reforming European Catholicism in the wake of the Protestant Reformation (the set book by Wallace deals with this on pp. 124–6). The Confederates negotiated only with the royalists (since they regarded themselves as subjects of the king seeking recognition for their religion).

Supporters of parliament were chiefly New English planters. Protestant regions of Ulster were controlled by Scots Presbyterians, reinforced by troops from Scotland under the command of George Munro, who co-operated uneasily with parliament's forces according to the state of relations in Scotland with the parliament in England. The principal royalist leaders were the earl of Ormond, a Protestant Old Englishman, and the earl of Inchiquin, a member of the important Gaelic Irish O'Brien family who, from 1644 to 1648, changed his allegiance to parliament.

For the most part, the king regarded Ireland as a potential provider of troops in England while the English parliament (much influenced by the propaganda around the 1641 rising) regarded it as an uncomfortable neighbour who might harbour supporters of the king and thus needed subduing. Two expeditions were sent by parliament before 1649, but neither made much difference to the situation there. At various times the royalists made truces with the Confederates, but these were denounced by the clerical wing of the Confederation.

Just as the divisions between the protagonists in Scotland related only partially to the divisions in England, so did those in Ireland. Just as the Covenanters established a kind of confessional state independent of the king, so, too, did the Confederation of Kilkenny. In both countries, wars were fought against England to preserve these gains.

It is clear that for many of those who took up arms in different parts of the British Isles, defence of religious beliefs and practices was paramount. For some, this included defending the religious justification for monarchy. Many combatants also believed fervently that God was on their side and viewed victories as signs of divine approval and defeats as signs of divine displeasure. But the course of the wars led to the evolution of new ideas both about religious liberty and about the nature of the state and the locus of power. The idea of a divine-right monarchy was irreparably damaged by events in all three nations.

Let us now look at the ways in which the population bore the cost of the war.

THE COST OF THE WAR

Mortality

One of the most extraordinary aspects of the Civil Wars is how it was possible to sustain for so long wars where all sides needed to raise money, men and provisions. The cost in terms of lives lost as a result of military actions has been estimated at around 84,000 for England and Wales for the period 1642–51, of whom two-thirds died in the First Civil War (1642–46)

(Woolrych, 2002, p. 335). Figures for Ireland are much more conjectural because the principal source is the 1641 depositions (see Unit 10). Disease – typhus, dysentery and the plague – accompanied armies and was rife in besieged cities, which accounted for further civilian lives. While the armies roamed the country, wartime civilian mortality seems to have been relatively localised. In most southern counties in England, for example, the mortality rate in the period 1642–46 was level with that before and after the war; but Berkshire experienced a sharp and unrepeated rise in 1642–46, probably accounted for by the passage of armies along the Thames valley between London and Oxford. The Oxfordshire town of Thame also had a mortality crisis in 1643, probably caused by typhus brought by parliamentary forces arriving preparatory to an attack on Oxford (Bell, 1990, p. 144). The experience of Thame was repeated in other parishes close to military engagements, where civilian mortality rose, though the numbers of *military* burials recorded is insignificant (Dils, 1989, p. 49).

Gentry

Let us now look at the experiences of two individual civilians. Many literate people believed themselves to be living through extraordinary times and kept journals.

EXERCISE	Turn to Anthology Document 3.16, 'Passages from Isabella and Roger Twysden's diaries, 1645', and read extract (a), Isabella Twysden's journal.

1   What is the balance between recording public events and private matters?

2   What can a document such as this tell a historian of the Civil Wars?

Spend about 20 minutes on this exercise.

SPECIMEN ANSWER	1 The journal is a complete mixture of the personal and the public. It is difficult to tell which of the individuals she names Lady Twysden knew personally. She may have known Archbishop Laud, because as archbishop of Canterbury he lived in Kent. The executions of the Hothams and Laud were nationally important events. Part of the purpose of the journal seems to have been to keep a record of the employment of the children's nurses and how much they were paid.

2   We learn something about the dissemination of news outside London and what events were considered to be significant (we do not know how Lady Twysden got to hear of what was happening in London – whether it was from letters, newsbooks or conversations with neighbours). Ordinary domestic life continued regardless of the war, but Lady Twysden had to take responsibility, in her husband's absence, for running the family's estate.

EXERCISE	Now turn to Anthology Document 3.16, 'Passages from Isabella and Roger Twysden's diaries, 1645', and read extract (b), Sir Roger Twysden's diary.

1   What do you notice about his wartime concerns?

2   Compare his writing and the content of his diary with that of his wife (both are in the original spelling)

Spend about 20 minutes on this exercise.

SPECIMEN ANSWER

1   Sir Roger was not directly involved in the fighting (at this time he was forty-eight years of age). His primary concerns were the welfare of his family: the birth of the child, his wife's travels, her need to get some payments from the estates and the attempt to get the fine reduced. While he was detained (under house arrest, rather than in prison), he pursued the antiquarian and legal interests common to many seventeenth-century gentlemen.

2   The spelling and expression are quite different. Though Sir Roger's spelling varies from modern spelling, it is consistent (for example, he writes 'knwe' instead of 'knew'). Isabella's is much more phonetic – it makes better sense if read aloud. The abbreviated form of Isabella's entries suggests someone without much time to spare and for whom penmanship may have been something of an effort, while Roger was plainly at ease with the written word.

DISCUSSION

By putting the two diaries together we learn a good deal more than either one of them can tell us on its own. We learn, for example, from Sir Roger's diary, that his wife dealt directly with the members of the parliamentary committee concerned with granting her an allowance.

We also see Sir Roger as a parliamentarian, not in the sense of a supporter of parliament in the war, but in the sense of someone who was a member of the political nation – a former MP who understood how parliamentary committees worked.

Note too, that the religious phraseology so commonly associated with supporters of parliament rises readily to his pen in his thanks for his wife's safe journey. This kind of language was shared by godly people on both sides of the divide over ceremonies and bishops.

EXERCISE

Go to the online *Oxford Dictionary of National Biography* (you will find a link to this on the course website) and look up Sir Roger Twysden. You can download or print this. What was the financial cost of the Civil War to him?

Spend about 20 minutes on this exercise.

SPECIMEN ANSWER

The City of London demanded £400 from him for their loan to parliament (he mentions this in his journal) despite being, as he argued, not a permanent resident of the city. His house contents were seized to meet this debt. His Kentish lands were sequestrated and the timber felled. To recover his lands he agreed to a fine of £3,000, which he could not afford to pay so the sequestration remained in effect. It was not until 1650 that he recovered his lands, having finally negotiated a fine of £1340 to recover them. In addition, he had to pay an assessment of £600, which was eventually reduced to £389 18s 6d.

DISCUSSION

Twysden was not an ardent royalist (he had refused to pay Ship Money), nor was he a particularly rich man. His annual income was assessed at £750, so the fines amounted to several years' income. He refused to join the king at Oxford in order to protect his family's property in Kent. However, his prewar career made him a notable figure and since his lands lay in a part of Kent that strongly supported parliament he had little chance of living out the war in obscurity. In addition to the forced loan and the fines, he was presumably charged with the monthly assessment tax.

Let us now look at the costs of some of the forces that were maintained during the war.

Armed forces

Though the great set-piece battles had a significant impact on the politics of the period, such engagements were relatively unusual. All over England, but especially in the Midlands, were garrisons, generally based on older fortified houses. These were usually manned by soldiers drawn from the surrounding area, who ventured out on skirmishes against forces from other similar garrisons. King and parliament developed similar systems of local administration to raise taxation, men and supplies. Parliament adopted the form of a weekly assessment levied on every £1 value of an individual's property provided the property was worth more than £10. Local officials appointed by the parliamentary committee for the administration of each county collected and recorded the assessments. One of the Wiltshire collectors, based at Great Chalfield garrison, noted that 'the country had liberty to pay in victual, hay, oats, or might work it out at the fortifications; whereby far the greater part was brought in such provisions as they could spare'(Pafford,1966, p. 45).

EXERCISE

Look now at Anthology Document 3.15, 'Supplying a provincial garrison', extracts (a) and (b), and answer the following questions.

1   What do you notice about the goods, labour and money *collected* (shown in extract (a))?

2   What do you notice about the goods *bought* for the garrison (shown in extract (b))?

3   Can we conclude anything about the impact of such a garrison on the local community?

Spend about 10 minutes on this exercise.

SPECIMEN ANSWER

1   The greatest value was money (£21 16s), contrary to the collector's observation that most people brought provisions. There was a large amount of cheese and grain (oats and wheat), and some malt. The arrears were surprisingly large – two-thirds of the total.

2   The disbursements for the garrison were for a miscellany of goods and services. There is no distinction between the wages bills (for the porter, the foot soldiers and the gunsmith), occasional payments for services (for work on the bulwarks, a guide, fetching Widow Somner's oxen, the spy and a messenger), military supplies (canon and musket baskets, bridles) and domestic supplies (capons, butter, eggs, beer, earthenware and salt).

3   Providing food, clothing and equipment for 200 men and fodder for 100 horses was no small matter. Men and mounts were usually recruited locally for such garrisons, depleting the local labour force. In addition, residents of surrounding

parishes had to find money, goods or labour to pay the assessment. But the garrison was also a paying consumer of local goods and services. It doesn't look as if it had to buy cheese or grain, but it was buying poultry and dairy products, and the amount of labour service it could call on was insufficient to do all the work needed on the fortifications so additional labourers had to be employed and paid.

1   Wiltshire was a county noted for cheese making and grain growing. The malt was used for making beer, the staple drink in the absence of safe water supplies. Only the poorest people tended to supply labour. The labour of the five men was calculated at 8d a day, the standard agricultural day-labourer's rate.

2   Many of the services the garrison required could probably be found locally; there were plenty of agricultural labourers. But gunsmithing was a skilled craft more usually associated with cities.

3   The assessment received at Great Chalfield was collected from about twenty-four parishes, including the market towns of Trowbridge, Melksham and Bradford-on-Avon, and fell far below the sums charged on each parish. There were few opportunities for local people to make large profits from providing goods and services to the garrison, but in other parts of the country, manufacturing arms, ammunition and clothing for the army was of some importance. There were some seasonal variations: for example, in June, the garrison was buying peas, beans, kale, salad and radishes, and wheat, the earlier supplies having presumably been exhausted.

Local garrisons and forces relied on local supplies; New Model Army forces, which could number at least 17,000 men, were often quartered on local households. The larger armies passed repeatedly through the same areas of the country and householders must have found it difficult to provide food and animal fodder in the quantities required. Contractors in London seem to have been used to provide arms, clothing and equipment – at least £450,000 was spent on these in London between 1638 and 1652 (Coates, 2004, p. 90). There were also major contractors who manufactured and transported bulk quantities of cheese and biscuit (Nusbacher, 2000, pp. 155–9). Coates estimates that a high proportion of the £4.25 million spent on the New Model Army went into the London economy to buy food for the troops (Coates, 2004, p. 91). It is clear that contractors for food, clothing and equipment for the armies had some difficulty in getting paid. The sums involved could be very large – Stephen Estwick issued £23,000-worth of clothing to the earl of Essex's soldiers in 1642 and was still owed half that sum in April 1643 (Coates, 2004, p. 93).

Plainly the need to produce and transport such goods had an impact on the economy of London, but Ben Coates, historian of London's Civil War economy, concludes that while arms were imported and manufacturing capacity expanded there is little evidence for the development of more capitalistic modes of production (Coates, 2004, pp. 92, 100). Nor did new trade and financial networks and mechanisms need to be established; the London livery companies continued and developed their control of the trades with which they had traditionally been associated.

THE STATE, 1649–60

The trial and execution of the king

While there was fighting in progress, it is hard to discern the role of the state: had the state actually disintegrated? Think back to the functions of the state identified in Unit 9. The law courts had more or less collapsed and almost all the administration was directed to military matters, especially to the raising of taxes to pay the many armies. If we look at the qualities identified as being those of a state – a set of institutions with its own personnel, including the means of violence and coercion, and having the monopoly of rule making within that territory – we can see that these had multiplied. There were the institutions of the king's administration in Oxford; parliament's administration in Westminster and Whitehall; the Covenanting administration in Edinburgh; the Catholic Confederation of Kilkenny; and the remnants of the English administration in Dublin. All of these ran some of the institutions that characterise a state, and several of them (the king in Oxford, parliament in Westminster and the Confederation of Kilkenny) conducted extensive negotiations with foreign powers; the Confederation even had a papal nuncio in residence.

But the test of statehood came with the decision to put Charles I on trial. By what right could the victorious parliament of England put the king of England and Wales, Scotland and Ireland on trial? Remember (Unit 10, p. 57) that the Scots had already declared the king to be *under* the law, but there was no such convention in England. And in any case, what legitimacy had a House of Commons originally elected in 1640 and reduced in membership from about 470 to around 200 MPs by Pride's Purge in December 1648? The House of Lords was now made up of only fifteen or so peers, of whom commonly fewer than ten sat to 'tell tales by the fireside in their House in the hope of more Lords to drive away the time' (quoted in Firth, 1910, p. 206). On 1 January 1649, the Commons, without a division, passed an ordinance to put the king on trial and appointed 150 commissioners (including six peers) to act as judge and jury. The following day, the ordinance was sent up to the Lords and was rejected by the twelve peers present.

EXERCISE

Look now at Anthology Document 3.17, 'The trial of Charles I', part (c), 'Parliament and king, 1649'. What are the implications of the vote of 4 January 1649 that parliament on 20 January ordered to be printed?

Spend about 15 minutes on this exercise.

SPECIMEN ANSWER

The House of Commons declared that, as it represented the people of England who were 'the original of all just power', it had supreme power in the land and could by itself make laws without king or lords.

The Commons thus, on its own, set in train the arrangements for the king's trial.

EXERCISE

Read Anthology Document 3.17, 'The trial of Charles I', part (a), 'Extracts from the trial proceedings'. What was the king's response to the charges made against him?

Spend about 15 minutes on this exercise.

SPECIMEN ANSWER

The king declined to answer the charges on the grounds that 'I would know by what power I am called hither', by what 'lawful authority'. Nevertheless, he attempted to debate with the court about the nature of his rights. He argued that he was a hereditary not an elective monarch, that he represented the people of England better than any High Court of Justice and that the Commons had no capacity as a law court.

DISCUSSION

The Commons, having already declared they were 'the supreme power in this nation', did not defend their actions. But they were scrupulous in procedural matters and collected depositions from witnesses to show the king's involvement in the war. There are two examples in Anthology Document 3.17, 'The trial of Charles I', part (b), 'Depositions taken against the king, 27–30 January 1649, extracts (i) and (ii).

The court decided on the king's guilt and sentenced him to be executed; look back to the start of this unit for the impact of that occasion. Parliament had then to deal with the consequences of the vacancy of the head of state. It was (as it still is) customary for the new monarch to be proclaimed at the same time as the old one was declared dead. So, between 27 and 30 January 1649, the Commons passed an Act to prohibit the declaration of a new king and, to give it force, ordered that the Commons' claims of 4 January be printed (see Anthology Document 3.17, part (c)). In effect, this meant that the monarchy had been abolished (an Act confirming this was passed on 17 March), and on 6 February the abolition of the Lords followed.

What became of the monarchy?

But all of this was an English affair. In Scotland, Charles I's eldest son Charles was told he would be recognised as king on the condition of his 'espousing God's cause', and in 1651 he was crowned in Scotland by the marquis of Argyle (not, as would have been the case in England, by an ecclesiastic). After hearing a sermon, Charles swore the National Covenant and the Solemn League and Covenant. A Scottish observer noted that 'There were many bonfires set forth in token of joy. His majesty, when he was crowned, was not anointed at all, because the Commission of the Kirk thought it to savour somewhat of superstition' (Lamont, 1830, pp. 26–7). In Ireland, the leading royal servant, the earl of Ormond, had concluded a truce with the Catholic Confederation of Kilkenny in December 1648, and the Ulster Scots had agreed to put themselves under his command. Charles II was proclaimed king in Ireland in February 1649.

Between 1649 and 1652, England, with an army led initially by Oliver Cromwell, embarked on wars of conquest in Ireland and then in Scotland. Ireland was chosen first, partly because of the danger posed by the uniting of two hitherto separate opponents of parliament, the Irish Catholic Confederation of Kilkenny and the royalists led by Ormond. Cromwell's own campaign in Ireland, the most dramatic engagements of which were the burning and destruction of Drogheda and Wexford, lasted from July 1649 until May 1650, but the country was not finally subdued until 1652. Irish prisoners taken at Drogheda and elsewhere were shipped to Barbados (as had been Scots prisoners taken at Preston and English prisoners taken at Colchester in the Second Civil War). Later plans to ship Irish boys and girls to Jamaica foundered because, as indentured servants, they were not considered to be sufficiently profitable by comparison with the African slaves whose transportation was just beginning (Corish, 1978, p. 363).

The constitution and the three kingdoms

For this section you will find it helpful to look at Table 11.1, later in this unit. During the years 1649–60, different experiments in government were tried. One of the most novel features was the introduction of a written constitution, unlike the ancient unwritten constitution of king in parliament. Another was the creation of a parliamentary union of England (with Wales), Scotland and Ireland – something that was not subsequently achieved until 1800.

The first written constitution, the Instrument of Government, was drawn up by General John Lambert and approved by the Council of Officers in December 1653; it vested power in a protector (Oliver Cromwell) and Council of State (of between thirteen and twenty-one members to be chosen from names put forward by parliament) whose actions parliament could veto. The protector had the power only to hold up legislation for twenty days; he had no power to veto it. The Humble Petition and Advice of 1657 was drawn up by a group of civilians and was intended to correct problems that had arisen in the implementation of the Instrument of Government and the troubles of the first two Protectorate parliaments. It introduced a second chamber as well as the Commons – a senate of nominated worthies; it increased the protector's powers over the council; it much increased the government's income; and it considerably limited the *de facto* religious toleration of the Instrument. It also invited Cromwell to assume the title of king (but not hereditary monarch) and to nominate his successor. He declined the first and did not avail himself of the second until September 1658, when he was dying. While the constitution contained many measures that greatly improved on anything of Charles I's reign, it failed to secure the support of the political nation and thus linked the Protectorate to the fortunes of the army.

During the administration of the Rump Parliament, some discussions about parliamentary union with Scotland took place, and (as you can see from Anthology Document 3.18, 'Scotland under the Commonwealth', part (b), 'The diary of John Lamont, 1652') the union was declared in 1652, but its first realisation was with Barebone's Parliament. The four Scots members were not dyed-in-the-wool Covenanters – they needed to have some sympathy with the prevailing Independent religious views of the majority of English members. The six Irish members were neither Irish nor religious radicals, but represented Protestant settlers and soldiers in Ireland. The union between England and Scotland was only formally enacted in 1657, and then without a proper form of assent by the Scottish people. In the Protectorate parliaments the Scots were under-represented, there being 400 English MPs and 30 Scots, leading a Scot to comment that the relationship was 'as when a poor bird is embodied into the hawk that hath eaten it up' (quoted in Donaldson, 1978, p. 344). However, in the later parliaments, the MPs were mainly Scots rather than Englishmen. In contrast, no Act of Union between England and Ireland was ever passed, and English authority over Ireland was exercised by the protector and Council of State rather than through the army officers who made up most of the thirty MPs.

Underlying the constitutional experiments was the army. It was the military who governed the sitting and dissolution of assemblies. When, in 1653, Cromwell dissolved the Rump Parliament he did so with the support of the Council of Officers, who proposed the scheme for an assembly whose 144 members (including four for Scotland and six for Ireland) they were to nominate from among religious congregations. This parliament is known by the name of one of its more obscure members – Praise-God Barebone. Before Barebone's Parliament met, Cromwell simply governed as commander-in-chief of the army. The military were behind the Instrument of Government. They protested against the intentions of the Humble Petition and Advice to increase civilian control and caused Richard Cromwell to dissolve his parliament; they recalled and expelled the Rump Parliament; General Monck, arriving from his command in Scotland, recalled the MPs who had been excluded by Pride's Purge in 1648, and opened negotiations with the exiled Charles II.

The state and the military

Two particular episodes illustrate the dependence of the state on the army. The first was the military occupations of Scotland and Ireland throughout the period and the second was what is known as the 'rule of the major-generals' (from October 1655 to January 1657).

Following the invasion of Scotland in 1650, and the defeat of the Scots by the New Model Army at Dunbar and Worcester, a military government was established in Scotland with a number of garrisons which were maintained until 1660, even though the administration was increasingly handed over to civilians. One particular consequence of the occupation was the idea that Scottish legal procedures should be assimilated with those of England (though for some time it was martial law that ruled).

EXERCISE

Read Anthology Document 3.18, 'Scotland under the Commonwealth', part (a), 'The diary of John Lamont, 1652', and part (b), 'The diary of John Nicoll, December 1651'.

What attitudes did both men have to the English occupation?

Spend about 15 minutes on this exercise.

SPECIMEN ANSWER

Nicoll noted the abolition of the Scottish courts and his comments suggest that the religious practices of the soldiers were only made tolerable by their good discipline. Lamont noted the proclamation of the union without consultation and the abolition of the Scots courts.

In Ireland, the suppression of resistance to the English parliamentary forces was more protracted and, though an administration was established in Dublin, it was not for several years that outlying resistance was overcome. The creation of a civilian administration was partly impeded by the appointment of Charles Fleetwood, a man whose talents were military rather than political, as commander-in-chief in 1652. Even after he was succeeded by Henry, Oliver Cromwell's son, the military aspect of England's government remained much more obvious in Ireland than in Scotland: there were over 20,000 of parliament's soldiers in Ireland in 1654, and even in 1658 there were 12,000.

The rule of the major-generals came about because of the failure of the Protectorate parliaments to agree on the terms of the Instrument of Government. Following Penruddock's royalist uprising of March 1655, the Council of State decided to appoint military governors (known as major-generals) to govern the twelve districts into which England and Wales were divided. Each major-general had powers to raise and direct new county militias for the peace and security of the district and to pay for them by levying a new tax on royalists, even those who had been quiescent, who possessed land worth £100 per annum or who had £1,500-worth or more of personal assets. This militarisation of the government of England and Wales did not involve large numbers of soldiers; indeed, the government had been trying since 1653 to reduce the size of the army and had already disbanded a significant number of soldiers. But it meant government by military officers in their capacity as members of the army rather than simply as agents of parliament. It was the most hated feature of the government of the Protectorate, and major-generals were reviled as tyrants.

EXERCISE

Read Anthology Document 3.19, 'The rule of the major-generals', which consists of two letters from Major-General Thomas Kelsey. What were Kelsey's greatest concerns?

Spend about 15 minutes on this exercise.

SPECIMEN ANSWER

In the first letter, Kelsey's concerns were with chasing up and disarming former royalists (delinquents and malignants), understandable in the light of Penruddock's rising, and with raising the decimation tax. In the second, his concerns were with the blasphemous statements of Richard Coppin and their influence on the troops at

Rochester. He also shows some concern for the public reputation of the administration, wanting to avoid slurs of persecution.

The rule of the major-generals brought to a head the uneasy relations between civilians and the military in the government. But removing the major-generals in 1657 did not solve any problems. One of the features of the 1650s was that anyone contemplating a restoration of civilian rule was conscious of the army waiting on the sidelines, and knew that without the army they could not govern. The final test came in 1658 with the death of Cromwell, when, although there was little change in the personnel of the administration, we might have expected a further advance towards civilian rule with a new protector. Richard Cromwell, Oliver's eldest son, was not a military man, but the army forced him to dissolve his parliament of 1659. Thereafter, the calling and dissolving of assemblies was in the hands of the army and, ultimately in the hands of General Monck, with whom Charles II was in correspondence in March 1660 before his return.

CONCLUSION

Table 11.1 summarises the most significant changes that took place in the state in the years 1642–60. You don't need to learn it by heart but you should use it as an aid to understanding the scale and the scope of the changes that took place over the revolutionary years.

You can see, for example, how a good many of the functions of the state existed in parallel until the early 1650s, when there was created a single polity, though not one with a uniform judiciary, church or local administration. Conrad Russell described Charles I as 'head of a multiple monarchy' (Russell, 2000, p. 82). Likewise, the state over which Cromwell and the Council of State presided was not a unitary state, but a multiple one. But while Russell attributes the breakdown of relations between the king and his subjects to Charles's attempts to impose uniformity on his kingdoms, it seems that the collapse of the Protectorate, of the republic, owed more to tensions between civilians and the military – to a crisis of legitimacy rather than to a failure of political processes.

The most striking feature of the years 1649–60 was that there existed a de facto republic even though Scotland and Ireland had not abolished the monarchy. In the course of the 1640s, there emerged a strain of republican thinking, often allied to radical Protestantism, but confessed republicanism was unusual and it is striking how rapidly objections to monarchical rule melted away with the prospect of a return to political stability.

Table 11.1   Changes in the state 1642–60

	England and Wales	Scotland	Ireland
Ruler	King Charles I until 30 January 1649 Oliver Cromwell, lord protector, December 1653 to September 1658 Richard Cromwell, lord protector, September 1658 to 1659 Council of State 1660	King Charles I until 30 January 1649 Charles II declared king in 1649 and crowned in 1651, but in exile from 1651 Role of head of state occupied by whoever was head of state in England 1651–60	King Charles I until 30 January 1649 Charles II declared king in February 1649 Role of head of state occupied by whoever was head of state in England 1649–60, but no formal act of union was passed
Legislature	House of Commons, 1640–53 (c.470 MPs; purged of c.200 MPs in 1648, known thereafter as the Rump) House of Lords, 1640–1649 (when abolished)	Scottish parliament (estates), 1636–41, 1644–47 (after 1640 met without royal authority). Bishops excluded from 1639. In the absence of the estates sitting, business was conducted by the Committee of Estates replacing the Committee of the Lords of the Articles Membership in 1641 was 56 nobles, 50 gentry and 54 burgesses	Irish Parliament (240 MPs, of whom 20% were Catholic before the rising of 1641), last sat in 1642 but was continued by prorogations until 1646 General Assembly of the Confederation of Kilkenny, 1642–49, controlled Catholic Ireland (9 meetings; c.250 members representing the same constituencies at the parliament, Catholic bishops, c.19 Catholic peers)
	Barebone's Parliament, July to December 1653 (134 MPs for England and Wales)	Barebone's Parliament, July to December 1653 (4 MPs for Scotland)	Barebone's Parliament, July to December 1653 (6 MPs for Ireland)
	1st Protectorate parliament, September 1654 to January 1655 (400 MPs for England and Wales)	1st Protectorate parliament, September 1654 to January 1655 (30 MPs for Scotland)	1st Protectorate parliament, September 1654 to January 1655 (30 MPs for Ireland, most of whom were army officers)
	2nd Protectorate parliament, September 1656 to February 1658 3rd Protectorate parliament, January to April 1659 Elected on a franchise of all adult males with real or personal estate valued at £200 except Catholics, abettors of the Irish rebellion Rump Parliament, May to October 1659 2nd recall of Rump, December 1659 Commons including members excluded in 1648, February to March 1660	2nd Protectorate parliament, September 1656 to February 1658 3rd Protectorate parliament, January to April 1659	2nd Protectorate parliament, September 1656 to February 1658 3rd Protectorate parliament, January to April 1659

Judiciary	Judges were appointed under the Great Seal of the Commonwealth	Court of Session lapsed in July 1651	After 1649, only Protestants could practise in the law courts.
	Church courts abolished 1646, regulatory functions taken over by JPs	Justice temporarily in hands of a committee of English army officers	Common law courts were revived after the war but senior legal officers were usually Englishmen
	Judicial functions of House of Lords lapsed with its abolition in 1649	May 1652, 8 commissioners of justice installed (5 English and 3 Scots). Heritable jurisdictions and baron courts (feudal courts) replaced by JPs	
	Attempts made to reform courts, especially Chancery	Senior judges by mid 1650s were mainly Scotsmen	
Executive	Royal Privy Council in Oxford until 1646	Privy Council lapsed July 1651 with collapse of royalists	Royal administration in Dublin, 1642–49. Ormond lord lieutenant 1643–60 (in exile 1650–60);
	Parliamentary Committee of Safety, 1642–43; Committee of Both Kingdoms (with Scots members), 1644–47; Derby House Committee, 1647–49	Covenanters' business was carried out by Committee of Estates and subcommittees, 1643–51. Some overlap in membership with Kirk's commission for public affairs	Lord Lisle appointed lord lieutenant by parliament, 1646–47
	Various Councils of State, 1649–60	October 1651 to July 1655, government conducted by 8 English military commissioners	Supreme council of the Confederation of Kilkenny over Catholic Ireland, 1642–49 (*c.*24 members)
	Parliamentary organisation of county committees extended into peacetime	July 1655, Council of State of 8 members	May 1650 to November 1651, Henry Ireton commander-in-chief; November 1651, Edmund Ludlow commander-in-chief; July 1655, Henry Cromwell commander-in-chief; November 1657, Henry Cromwell lord deputy; October 1658, Henry Cromwell lord lieutenant; June 1659, Cromwell replaced by English parliamentary commissioners; July 1659, Edmund Ludlow commander-in-chief; December 1659, Council of Officers assumed control
	1655–57, Major-Generals for each county		
Foreign policy	During the war, directed both from London and from Oxford. From 1649, directed by Council of State and protector in Whitehall. Foreign states began to recognise the new regime and to send ambassadors to London, despite the embarrassment of a royal court in exile	Directed from Whitehall	Directed from Whitehall Confederation of Kilkenny, 1642–49, had papal nuncio in attendance and negotiated with foreign Catholic powers

Defence	Royal Council of War in Oxford; field army; local forces under Commissions of Array and parish officers. Some forces from Ireland (mainly English settlers) Parliament's field armies; local forces at first under lords lieutenant and deputy lieutenants, later under county committees. From April 1645, field armies and some local forces combined into the New Model Army under the command of Sir Thomas Fairfax. Locally raised armies continued to outnumber the New Model Army until 1648	Covenanting army led by Leslie and Callandar Royalist army led by Montrose, 1643–6 After 1651, army of occupation controlled from Westminster and based on 5 principal Scottish forts. 18,000 soldiers in 1654 reduced to establishment of 10,500 by 1657	Forces commanded by English administration at Dublin Castle; some raised by noblemen for king; forces of Confederation of Kilkenny; forces from Scotland commanded by George Munro; forces sent by parliament After 1650, army directed from Dublin Castle by advisers from Westminster. 34,000 men in 1652, 23,000 in 1654, around 16,000 from 1655
Taxation	Levied from areas occupied by royalists and parliamentarians during wartime Instrument of Government, 1653, provided for revenue sufficient to support army of 30,000 men, a fleet and £200,000 per annum to support civil government, all other needs to be funded by parliamentary vote	Monthly assessment on real and personal estate; did not support costs of administration and army	Military supported by payments from England
Church	Westminster Assembly of Divines appointed in 1643 to produce new church settlement to conform to Solemn League and Covenant. Presbyterian system partially implemented. Partial system of Presbyterian assemblies set up. Use of Anglican services and Prayer Book proscribed. From 1649, freedom of conscience except for Catholics and Anglicans, but exponents of extreme views (such as denying the divinity of Christ or flouting all God's laws) prosecuted. Proposal to abolish tithes not enacted	General Assembly of the Kirk until 1653, when dissolved because it had no authority from new parliament in London Military administration in favour of toleration of most forms of Protestantism. Some radical sects established by English soldiers Protestors (radical Covenanters) in sympathy with military occupation, but Resolutioners (who had supported Engagement) more numerous	Protestant church administered by secular administration in Dublin, main efforts addressed to English garrisons; some Church of Scotland congregations. Catholic priests to be executed under Act for Settling Ireland 1652 Catholic Ireland administered by Catholic bishops during period of Confederation of Kilkenny, 1642–49, with intervention from papal nuncio

REFERENCES

Abbott, W.C. (ed.) (1937) *The Writings and Speeches of Oliver Cromwell*, 4 vols, Oxford, Oxford University Press.

Bell, J. (1990) 'The mortality crisis in Thame and east Oxfordshire', *Oxfordshire Local History*, vol. 3, pp. 137–52.

Coates, B. (2004) *The Impact of the English Civil War on the Economy of London*, Aldershot, Ashgate.

Corish, P. (1978) 'The Cromwellian regime, 1650–60' in Moody, T.W., Martin, F.X. and Byrne, F.J. (eds) *A New History of Ireland*, vol.3, *Early Modern Ireland 1534–1691*, Oxford, Clarendon Press.

Dictionary of National Biography on CD-ROM (1988) 'Ussher', Oxford, Oxford University Press.

Dils, J. (1989) 'Epidemics, mortality, and the civil war in Berkshire 1642–6', *Southern History*, vol. 11, pp. 40–52.

Donaldson, G. (1978) *Scotland: James V – James VII*, Edinburgh History of Scotland, vol. 3, Edinburgh, Oliver and Boyd.

Firth, C.H. (1910) *The House of Lords During the Civil War*, London, Longman.

Gardiner, S.R. (1893), *History of the Great Civil War 1642–1649*, 4 vols, London: Longmans Green.

Lamont, J. (1830) *The Diary of Mr John Lamont of Newton 1649–71*, Edinburgh, Maitland Club.

Macinnes, A. (1990) 'The Scottish constitution: the rise and fall of oligarchic centralism' in Morrill, J. (ed.) *The Scottish National Covenant in its British Context*, Edinburgh, Edinburgh University Press, pp. 106–33.

Morrill, J.S. (1974) *Cheshire 1630–1660: County Government and Society During the English Revolution*, Oxford, Oxford University Press.

Morrill, J.S. (1976) *The Revolt of the Provinces*, London, George Allen and Unwin.

Nusbacher, A.J.S. (2000) 'Civil supply and the civil war: supply of victuals to the New Model Army on the Naseby campaign', *English Historical Review*, vol. 115, pp. 145–60.

Pafford, J.H.P. (ed.) (1966) *Accounts of the Parliamentary Garrisons of Great Chalfield and Malmesbury 1645–46*, Wiltshire Record Society, vol. 2.

Russell, C. (2000) 'The British problem and the English civil war' in Gaunt, P. (ed.) *The English Civil War*, Oxford, Blackwell, pp. 79–103. (First published in *History*, 72, 1987).

Russell, C. (1990) *The Causes of the English Civil War*, Oxford, Oxford University Press.

Vicars, J. (1644) *Jehovah Jireh. God in the Mount*, London.

Wedgwood, C.V. (1971) *The Trial of Charles I*, London, Fontana.

Woolrych, A. (2002) *Britain in Revolution, 1625–1660*, Oxford, Oxford University Press.

Anne Laurence

INTRODUCTION

If the symbolic moment that defined the period 1642–60 was the execution of the king, symbolic moments that define the period covered by this unit (1660–91) are two royal landings: that of King Charles II at Dover on 23 May 1660 and that of William of Orange (not yet King William) at Torbay on 5 November 1688. These two events represent the fundamental change that had taken place as a result of the Civil Wars: that kings ruled on sufferance from their subjects. They represent both the fact that Charles and William were invited to come, but also that two kings – Charles I and James II – had been removed: Charles I by execution, James II by his flight. But these two moments were essentially English moments. The events that one might choose as defining moments in the histories of Scotland and Ireland represent the more troubled postwar histories of those countries.

In Scotland, William and Mary were proclaimed king and queen on 11 April 1689, but it was perhaps the massacre of thirty-eight Highlanders at Glencoe on 13 February 1691 that defined the difficulty William had in subduing Scotland, not merely because of Highlanders' support for the departed King James, but also because of the endemic fighting and feuding in those regions of the country.

In Ireland, which King James used as his base for trying to recover his position, the defining moment might be the battle of the Boyne (1 July 1690), commemorated in many pictures of William (see Figure 12.1). Another episode that continues to resonate, year after year, in the public display of Northern Ireland is the siege of Derry. The gates of the city were closed against James II's Catholic forces by thirteen apprentice boys on 7 December 1688. The siege of the city began in April 1689 and lasted 105 days. The Catholic counterpart, the defence of Limerick, is celebrated in a traditional dance.

WHAT WAS RESTORED?

Charles II (1630–1685) was declared king in Scotland and Ireland when his father was executed in 1649. He was invited to return to England as monarch in 1660 and resumed the kingship of all three kingdoms. His heir was his Catholic brother James. Charles vigorously opposed a plan to upset the hereditary succession by installing his illegitimate but Protestant son James, duke of Monmouth, as heir instead.

Figure 12.1   William III on horseback, late seventeenth century, English delftware, 7.6 x 35.5 cm. Fitzwilliam Museum, Cambridge. Photo: Fitzwilliam Museum, Cambridge. Depictions of the victorious Protestant William appeared in many guises. One of the most popular was on painted Delftware pottery, the fashion for which came from the Netherlands. This image was reproduced frequently on large dishes. It was transposed and adapted from an engraving by Cornelis van Dalen of Charles I entering Edinburgh.

In this unit we shall explore the consequences of the restoration of the monarchy and consider why it was that some of those matters unresolved in 1660 could not be settled until James II had departed and William and Mary installed as monarchs, and why it was that William's arrival was greeted in a rather more muted fashion than Charles's. In the course of this unit we shall consider:

- how the restoration of the monarchy was put into effect
- how opposition developed under Charles II and James II

- the nature and extent of the Glorious Revolution
- how we may view these events through the themes of the course
- what the revolution was
- how historians can use statistics and how they can manipulate them through a spreadsheet, using the example of the ecclesiastical census of 1676 known as the Compton Census – you will need to install and work on the CD-ROM for this.

On the face of it, the decision to invite Charles II to return solved the problem of who governed the country. No longer was there a contest between the military and parliament as to who controlled the head of state. Now there was a head of state who would technically rule 'in parliament' and who would be responsible for summoning the military in case of national danger. Abraham Cowley's verse extravagantly celebrated the king's arrival:

> All England but one bonfire seems to be,
> One Etna shooting flames into the sea.
> *Ode Upon His Majesties Restoration and Return*

While the diarist John Evelyn wrote on 3 May 1660 'Praised be for ever the Lord of Heaven, who only doeth wondrous things, because his mercy endureth for ever' (Evelyn, n.d., p. 321). But, welcome as Charles II was, many vital matters were left unresolved. What was most pressing differed from kingdom to kingdom. In England and Scotland, it was the church; in Ireland, it was land. In all three kingdoms, the relations of the monarch with parliament were ill defined and the extent of his extra-parliamentary powers was unclear.

Charles II was invited to return by a group of English notables; the Scots and the Irish were not consulted about the Restoration, and it was the support of the English military (the army in Scotland commanded by General George Monck) that assured Charles II's arrival. After the dissolution of the Rump in March 1660, a convention was summoned (known as a convention because it had called itself; it had not been summoned by the king). It was elected on the franchise used for the Long Parliament, rather than that used for the Protectorate parliaments, and thus contained only representatives for England and Wales. Before it met, Charles II issued what is now known as the Declaration of Breda.

EXERCISE

Read Anthology Document 3.20, 'Extract from the Declaration of Breda, 4 April 1660'. What powers did Charles claim for himself and what did he leave to parliament?

Spend about 20 minutes on this exercise.

SPECIMEN ANSWER

Charles referred to himself as 'defender of the faith', which implies that he regarded himself as head of the Church of England, and to the 'restoration' of 'king, peers and people to their just, ancient and fundamental rights'. He claimed the right to issue a general pardon. He also claimed the right to allow 'liberty to tender consciences', implying religious toleration.

This skilful document left to parliament decisions that were bound to be controversial: the extent of liberty to tender consciences; title to land bought or otherwise acquired during the 1640s and 1650s; and the payment of the army.

Meanwhile, the executive in London continued to rule Scotland and Ireland. The Restoration in Scotland began properly when the king nominated members to a Scots Privy Council (many of whom were Covenanters who had redeemed themselves by supporting the Engagement with Charles I in 1647 or by their opposition to the invading parliamentary forces in 1650–51). The Scottish estates, nobles and representatives of the burghs, did not meet until January 1661 to legislate for the new dispensation. The equivalent to the king appointing members of the Scots Privy Council was in Ireland the appointment of lords justices and a lord lieutenant (General Monck) and deputy; the Irish parliament met in May 1661.

England and Wales

We talk about the *restoration* of the monarchy in 1660 but, apart from Charles II returning from exile, to what extent was pre-Civil-War society reinstated? The House of Commons was restored on the old franchise and the House of Lords reassembled with bishops. All legislation passed after 1641 was declared null and void: everything that had had Charles I's assent was retained, notably the statutes that righted the most pressing grievances of the eleven years' personal rule, such as the abolition of the prerogative courts, feudal dues and prerogative taxes such as Ship Money. The most significant new regulation was the 1664 Triennial Act, which required parliament to meet every three years but not necessarily that a new parliament be called.

Many loyal royalists hoped that there would be some material restitution for their losses, but pragmatism ruled the day. In England, royalists who had forfeited their estates received compensation, while those who had sold their estates to pay fines (the majority) were not. Many royalists were in a similar situation to that of Sir Roger Twysden, of having had to pay swingeing fines rather than having their estates expropriated. The lands of the king, bishops, and deans and chapters that had been confiscated, sold and used to fund the Commonwealth were restored to their previous owners, the royal lands yielding an income of about £100,000 a year.

While only regicides, those responsible for the 1641 rebellion in Ireland and a few others were exempted from a general pardon, former supporters of parliament were justified in thinking that it was on the subject of religion that the king's supporters exacted their revenge. Despite Charles II's wishes, the parliament that met in 1661 and was finally dissolved in 1678 passed a succession of laws (known as the Clarendon Code) against Protestant nonconformity. In 1662, all clergy were required to assent to the new Book of Common Prayer (including the Thirty-Nine Articles) with the result that some 2,000 ministers left their livings. These were banned from preaching or living within five miles of their old parishes. Meetings for religious worship outside the established church were prohibited and anyone refusing to take the oath of allegiance was excluded from municipal corporations.

Scotland

> The application of the term 'restoration' to the period after 1660 misrepresents the nature of Scottish political and ecclesiastical life in those years. The monarchy was restored and the machinery of government in parliament, privy council and the judicature was again much as it had been before the outbreak of the covenanting revolt. But behind these externals, many essentials were different from what they had been under Charles I, and in so far as the revolt against that monarch had been aristocratic and anti-clerical it found its fulfilment rather than its negation under Charles II.
>
> (Donaldson, 1978, p. 358)

Donaldson's summary of the effect of the Restoration suggests that, for the Scots, a simple return to the status quo of the 1630s would not suffice. Though bishops were restored to the Church of Scotland, the general policy was to reinstate the church as it had been under King James VI and I, rather than as it had become under King Charles. While this was acceptable to many Scots, to the radical wing of the Covenanters, especially strong in south-west Scotland, who abhorred the Engagement with Charles I, it confirmed their alienation and some 270 ministers left the Church of Scotland rather than acknowledge bishops and repudiate the covenants.

A nostalgic Covenanting minister wrote of the time up to the Restoration:

> At the king's return every parish had a minister, every village had a school, every family almost had a Bible, yes, in most of the country all the children of age could read the scriptures ... I have lived many years in a parish where I never heard an oath ... Nobody complained more of our church government than our taverners, whose ordinary lamentation was, their trade was broke, people were become so sober.
>
> (Fyfe, 1928, pp. 242–3)

The Act Recissory abolished all laws passed since 1633, removing both Covenanting reforms and the most obnoxious of Charles I's legislation. Charles II turned to aristocrats and landlords to govern Scotland. It was thus necessary for him to rely on a group of men many of whom had been committed opponents of his father as moderate Covenanters. This was a notable contrast with England, where those aristocrats who gathered round the court had Anglican and royalist credentials.

Ireland

The Irish convention was summoned in Dublin by a group of English officers. It was these people who were to be best rewarded by the terms of the Restoration, disappointing the hopes of members of the Catholic Confederation of Kilkenny who thought that, because they had protested their faithfulness to the monarchy, the king would recognise their loyalty in tangible form. It was a combination of land and religion that dominated the Restoration settlement in Ireland, but land proved much the most intractable subject.

The Church of Ireland was restored and Catholic hopes of toleration were quickly dashed, though, as in England, the extent of persecution fluctuated. A pressing problem was that of nonconformity (primarily Scots Presbyterians in Ulster). During the 1650s, there had been a tendency to assume that any Protestant minister was preferable to a Catholic, so a very wide range of people had served the Protestant ministry. From 1666, all clergy had to conform to an Act of Uniformity requiring the use of the Book of Common Prayer and episcopal ordination for clergy. The Presbyterians in Ulster greeted the return of Church of Ireland bishops with dismay, and a good many clergy were ejected. They were also affected by the religious turmoil in Scotland.

The Catholics' chief concern was not the religious settlement, from which they knew they could expect nothing once it became apparent that there was no chance of toleration, but the land settlement. In Ireland, the criteria for judging how to allocate land after the Restoration were utterly different from those used in England. Much Irish land had been confiscated from Catholic rebels and granted to English settlers. Some of this had been in the form of direct grants, some had been in the form of debentures issued to English parliamentary soldiers in lieu of pay. In fact, few soldiers took their allocations of land; instead, they sold their debentures chiefly to people who already had some interest in Ireland. So, while there was a considerable redistribution of land from Catholics and Protestant royalists to Protestant supporters of parliament, the population of Protestants was not greatly enlarged. The principle of the Restoration land settlement was simple. It was to prefer Protestant landowners to Catholic, so lands were restored to Protestant royalists and a few 'innocent papists'. But the terms were difficult to implement, and several additional Acts had to be passed to effect them, because allowing Protestants to retain their land and meeting the claims of royalists and worthy Catholics proved impossible with the amount of land available.

EXERCISE	From which quarters in the British Isles might Charles have expected opposition?
	Spend about 10 minutes on this exercise.
SPECIMEN ANSWER	In England, from royalists disappointed by the lack of restitution of their property, and from Protestant nonconformists; in Scotland, from former Covenanters; in Ireland, from Catholics who regarded themselves as loyal to the monarchy and from Presbyterians.

As we shall see, few of these groups, with the exception of the Covenanters in Scotland, were to cause much difficulty. Rather, opposition came from people who might reasonably have been supposed to be Charles's supporters.

OPPOSITION

Charles II: England

Charles had a good political nose for survival and had no intention of being sent on his travels again. For much of his reign he put up with the opposition of nonconformists who were not, in the main, politically dangerous: most of them simply aspired to freedom of worship and to being recognised as citizens. In any case, they amounted to no more than about 5 per cent of the population. Only Quakers had been singled out for particular attention under the terms of the Clarendon Code. A rising of the radical sect called the Fifth Monarchy Men in 1661, and the Farnley Wood Plot of 1663 by a group of Presbyterians, gave the government no real cause for concern, but the administration was extremely responsive to rumour, and news of the activities of regicides in exile on the continent was sufficient to cause ripples in England.

The greatest subject for rumour was Catholic activity. It was Catholics who were, both directly and indirectly, to cause Charles most difficulty. Sympathetic to them – it was rumoured that even if he was not a secret Catholic during his lifetime, he made a deathbed conversion – he wanted on grounds of both tolerance and expediency to alleviate their position. But English prejudices about the absolutist ambitions of the king of France and his influence over his cousin Charles II flourished and were fed by tales of a Jesuit plot behind Great Fire of London (1666). J.R. Jones suggests that 'the Catholic church alone offered a clear, coherent and comprehensive challenge to every aspect of the established order' (Jones, 1978, p. 200). And there is no doubt that anti-Catholicism provided a suitable banner behind which Protestants of all shades of opinion could unite to heal the rifts of the 1640s and 1650s. In point of fact, there can have been little real risk since Catholics formed no more than 2 per cent of the population.

Three episodes raised particular anti-Catholic fury. The first was in 1672, when Charles, as a result of secret negotiations for a financial subsidy from Louis XIV of France, issued a Declaration of Indulgence, suspending the operation of the laws against Catholics and, incidentally, against nonconformists. Both judges and Commons objected to the legality of the measure. Charles had to withdraw the Indulgence and agree to the Test Act, which required all office holders not only to swear allegiance to the king and recognise that he was head of the church but also to provide documentary proof that they had taken the Anglican sacraments. The Test Act led to the second episode, when it was revealed, in 1673, that James, duke of York, Charles's brother and heir to the throne, had converted to Catholicism. This had no immediate consequences, not least because James's heirs were his two Protestant daughters, but the prospect of a Catholic ruler was destabilising. The third episode was an outstanding example of the power of rumour: the Popish Plot. In 1678, plans for a supposed Jesuit plot to assassinate the king were revealed to the government. Neither the revealers of the plot nor anyone else associated with it had any credibility, nor was there any foundation to the revelation. But such was the power of anti-Catholic feeling that for some months fears gripped the population, including parliament. These fears gave grounds for a proposal to exclude James, duke of York, from the succession to the throne and install as heir in his place, James, duke of Monmouth, Charles's illegitimate son. Charles was implacably opposed to setting aside the succession, not least because to allow inheritance by an illegitimate child would be to cause major difficulties for many propertied families. Bills were introduced in parliament in 1680 and 1681. The first was defeated in the House of Lords and the second was lost when Charles dissolved parliament.

What also aroused anxiety was not a religious matter, but a constitutional one. In 1662, Charles, seeing the unforgiving temper of parliament and the unlikelihood of achieving religious toleration through statute, issued a Declaration of Indulgence to suspend the operation of the laws against Protestant dissenters and Catholics. He was persuaded to withdraw this by the judges who doubted its legality. They had not changed their minds when, in 1672, he issued a second Declaration; this time both judges and parliament expressed their view that laws could only be suspended by statute. No one doubted that he had the power to dispense a few individuals from the operation of such a law, but suspending a law tested the extent of the king's powers. Although the suspending power was contested, the king's unchallenged power to dissolve parliament gave him very considerable control. Whether Charles's use of these devices shows tendencies towards absolutism is questionable.

We saw in Unit 10 how ecclesiastical visitations were used to keep track of the religion and morality of the population. Such visitations continued to be conducted in the Restoration church, but rather more intermittently. Charles II's lord treasurer, beset by anxieties about the strength of the Church of England in the face of all these rumours, seems to have been behind the decision of the archbishop of Canterbury, Gilbert Sheldon, to commission an ecclesiastical survey, 'the counting of noses', in 1675. Lord Treasurer Danby evidently wanted to persuade the king of the need to continue to support the Church of England by demonstrating through statistics that it had the support of the majority of the population. The Compton Census, as it is called (after Henry Compton, bishop of London), was sent round to all parishes in England, who were asked to record the number of people in each parish, the number of popish recusants (Catholics) and the number of Protestant nonconformists.

This national survey is of great importance because, apart from the figures for each religious group, it allows estimates of the population to be made for an era before censuses. However, it is not a simple source to use: in some parishes, the clergyman or church warden counted families or households rather than individuals; there was no clear guidance about the age at which people should be included (usually anyone over the age of 16); many dissenters may not have been included because they sometimes attended Anglican services. However, this is not a reason for not using the source, but a reason for trying better to understand it.

> **CD-ROM exercise**
>
> To see how historians can use material as this, you should now work on the CD-ROM. You should start by going to the *Media Guide* for instructions on installing the spreadsheets and on how to get started. On the CD-ROM are tutorials taking you through the statistics. This work (together with the exercise below) is likely to take you about 4 hours. It will prepare you for further work in Block 5.

EXERCISE

Now that you have worked through the figures for the Compton Census and seen the proportions of Catholics and nonconformists, consider why the activities of Catholics and nonconformists were so conspicuous.

EXERCISE

England was still a confessional state with an established church. The members of its government and parliament after the Test Act had to be practising members of that church. So it was still possible to equate Protestant or Catholic dissent from the Church of England with disloyalty, even though Charles II made no claims to divine right.

DISCUSSION

All the laws about church attendance that had been in force in Charles I's reign remained on the statute book and were reinforced by the legislation of the Clarendon Code. The church courts, which had been responsible for prosecutions for non-attendance at church, had not regained their prewar effectiveness and most prosecutions were under the Clarendon Code laws. But one prewar anxiety that had not gone away was that of continental Catholicism and its associations with absolutism. Louis XIV's actions were watched with interest and his control of the government of France and his territorial ambitions were viewed with suspicion.

Charles II: Scotland and Ireland

In Scotland, the Covenanters who refused to accept the reinstatement of bishops were forbidden to meet outside the official services of the Church of Scotland by the Act against conventicles, while former ministers were prevented from living within 20 miles of their former flocks. In the south-west, where conventicles were particularly common, military force was used to break up meetings and enforce the payment of fines. The Pentland Rising and the defeat of Covenanters in 1666 at Rullion Green led to a more conciliatory policy (though many rebels were shipped to Barbados). In 1669 and 1672, a number of excluded Presbyterian ministers were reinstated with the result that the Covenanting opposition lost its single-minded focus. But during the period 1674–79, repression was renewed with a law that required landlords and masters to take responsibility for the religious conformity of their tenants and employees. Widespread opposition in the south-west led to the imposition of the Highland Host in 1678, under which soldiers were quartered on recalcitrant communities. In 1679, the Covenanters assassinated the archbishop of St Andrews and rose in armed rebellion; they were defeated at Bothwell Brig (22

June 1679) by the king's forces under the command of his illegitimate son, the duke of Monmouth. Further repression took place in the early 1680s, partly in response the emergence of a radical group known as Cameronians, who disowned the king and engaged in guerrilla warfare. Like the Catholic fury in England, the Covenanting fury in Scotland made more noise than action, but nevertheless was deeply divisive.

The 1681 Test Act required anyone elected or appointed to office to acknowledge the royal supremacy of the Church of Scotland. But no attempt was made in Scotland to set aside the succession of James, duke of York, for that of James, duke of Monmouth. Had the any of the English Exclusion Bills passed, the duke of York would have remained heir to the Scottish throne.

In Ireland, initially the Church of Ireland commanded all official support, but in the course of the 1660s there was substantial toleration of Catholics provided they demonstrated that they were loyal to the king, as many of the Irish aristocracy did. Irish Catholic churchmen were caught up in the anti-Catholic fury generated by the Popish Plot, but the Presbyterians lived peaceably.

James II and VII

> **James II and VII** (1633–1701) was Charles II's younger brother. In 1660, he married Anne Hyde, daughter of Charles II's minister the earl of Clarendon. The couple had two daughters, Mary, who married her cousin Prince William of Orange, and Anne, who married George, a Danish prince. Anne Hyde died in 1671 and, having converted to Catholicism in 1673, James married the Catholic Princess Mary of Modena, who gave birth to a son in 1688. Between 1679 and 1682 he lived in Scotland. Following his flight in 1688, he lived in exile in France.

James II and VII's accession in 1685 prompted Monmouth's rising in the south-west of England. During his brief reign, James managed to turn many of the most loyal supporters of the Anglican Church and the Stuart monarchy into his opponents. He confirmed fears about the dangers of Catholicism and reminded everyone of the constitutional infractions of his father, Charles I. He had come to the throne in a very strong position in England, for his brother's reform of municipal corporations, to influence parliamentary elections, ensured that members of James's first parliament were unprecedentedly compliant; yet within three years he provoked a revolution.

He appointed Catholic officers to the army raised against Monmouth; he secured a judgement allowing him to dispense individuals from the Test Act; he suspended the English penal laws against Catholics and nonconformists with Declarations of Indulgence in 1687 and 1688; he attempted to get Magdalen College, Oxford, to accept a Catholic president. These measures roused, one by one, the Anglican, judicial and parliamentary establishment. Seven Anglican bishops, who had petitioned against the order to read the Declaration of Indulgence from the pulpit, were prosecuted for seditious libel; senior judges who repeatedly found against his right to suspend laws were dismissed; and the fellows of Magdalen College were deprived of their fellowships.

> **Archibald Campbell, 9th earl of Argyll** (executed 1685) was a great territorial magnate in the Highlands and associated with the radical Covenanters. He was prosecuted for various crimes which had primarily to do with his political influence in the Highlands. Having escaped, he led a rising against James II and VII in 1685 and was executed.

James had effectively been ruling Scotland from 1681, but at his accession a Highland rising led by the earl of Argyll, and loosely connected with Monmouth's rising, broke out. James's first parliament took a strong line against the rebellious Covenanters and declared attendance at conventicles (illegal religious assemblies) punishable by death. He introduced Catholics into a number of important positions in the country and announced that as parliament would not co-operate in giving Catholics freedom of worship, he would use his prerogative. His first measure for religious toleration in Scotland was confined to Catholics and Quakers, but a second one (1687) extended freedom of worship in private houses to non-Church-of-Scotland Presbyterians (i.e. Covenanters). James was strongly opposed in the Privy Council and by the Church of Scotland – two bishops were sacked for their opposition and anti-Catholic violence broke out in Edinburgh.

James's accession was 'received with joy by Irish Catholics, and with corresponding gloom by Protestants' (Simms, 1978, p. 478). But James also shared English prejudices against the Irish and regarded a Protestant government, and especially the ownership of land by Protestants, as the guarantee of English and thus royal power in Ireland. However, he did grant a number of commissions to Catholics in the Irish army and advanced the fortunes of the Catholic Richard Talbot, earl of Tyrconnell. Tyrconnell purged the army of Protestant rank and file and replaced them with Catholics. By 1687, the majority of judges and privy councillors in Ireland were Catholics. Catholics were installed as county sheriffs, responsible for parliamentary elections, ensuring that the next Irish House of Commons would be predominantly Catholic.

These measures were distasteful to Irish Protestants – both Anglicans and Presbyterians – as they excluded them from positions of power, influence and profit, but they were not actively damaging. James's policy of leaving Church of Ireland vacancies unfilled and using the income to subsidise Catholic clergy roused complaints. But what created a party of opposition to James was the rumour that the land settlement was to be altered to give Catholics sufficient land to secure them in the face of a possible Protestant succession on James's death. The rumour was given substance in 1688, when it was proposed that half of the Cromwellian land grants should be revoked in favour of Catholics, but that it was not at that moment expedient to hold a parliament in Ireland to enact this reform.

Revolt

It was the English whose dissatisfaction with James II was so great that it stimulated a group of English notables to think the unthinkable and open negotiations with Prince William of Orange, husband of James II's elder daughter Mary. Or was it unthinkable? Once one king had been despatched, doing it again seemed a distinct (though undesirable) possibility. The critical event was the birth of a son to King James and his queen in 1688 – a son who would be brought up as a Catholic, removing the prospect of a return to Protestant monarchy at James's death. Then, in October 1688, James ordered four regiments from Ireland to England. Not only were the troops disorderly but they raised ghosts of Charles I's use of Irish forces and of the unrestrained use of the royal prerogative. By themselves, these events might not have precipitated the invitation to William; it was the record of James's intransigence and insensitivity to his subjects' worries that made this the occasion.

It is arguable that many of the political and religious difficulties experienced by Charles II and James II arose from unfinished business at the Restoration. But William's keenness to secure England as an ally in his European venture against France made him an enthusiast for approaches from England. He had been in touch with a number of leading English politicians for some years before seven leading politicians wrote to him to propose that he would be supported if he led an expedition to England to secure a free parliament.

> **William of Orange** (1650–1702) succeeded his father, William II, as prince of Orange and ruler in the Netherlands, and was leader of the coalition of European states opposing Louis XIV's plans to extend France's territorial borders. He was a nephew of Charles II and James II, and married James's eldest daughter, Mary. In 1688, by invitation, he arrived in England and was declared monarch jointly with his wife. He subdued Scotland and Ireland. He used his position as king to continue to pursue military campaigns against Louis XIV of France. After Mary's death in 1694, he was declared king in his own right. See Figure 12.2.

Figure 12.2   Wax likenesses of William III and Mary II from Westminster Abbey, his modelled from life, hers from her death mask. Photo: © Dean and Chapter of Westminster

FOR WHOM WAS THE GLORIOUS REVOLUTION EITHER GLORIOUS OR A REVOLUTION?

William of Orange's arrival at Torbay was not greeted with the elation shown on Charles II's return. John Evelyn recorded on 5 November 1688 'These are the beginnings of great sorrow, unless God in his mercy prevent it by some happy reconciliation of all dissentions amongst us' (Evelyn, n.d., pp. 660). But for many English people, his arrival was a relief from the threat of popish and arbitrary rule.

England

William's arrival in England led to a speedy settlement; a convention declared the throne vacant, offered William and Mary the throne, and drew up the Declaration of Rights, later passed as the Bill of Rights. Most of the required legislation was passed during the year following: confirming the ascendancy of Protestantism; requiring that holders of elected positions and government offices take Anglican communion; and offering toleration (through the Toleration Act) without civil rights to Protestant dissenters. The Mutiny Act declared that a standing army might only be kept in peacetime with the consent of parliament. By the time that William's first parliament met in 1691, constitutional matters had been settled on a pragmatic basis and without bloodshed. But it could not be said that William's rule was secure in either Scotland or Ireland.

One transformation that William's reign achieved was that both monarch and people were united in regarding Louis XIV's France as the enemy. For William, one of the most appealing aspects of the English crown was that he could bring England into the anti-French alliance. Both Charles II and James II had wanted to conduct a pro-French foreign policy, which was much opposed by parliament, and both kings received substantial financial subsidies from Louis as the price of staying out of Europe. It would be difficult to claim by this time that there was any real sense of a Protestant alliance, though it happened that a good many of the states lined up against France happened to be Protestant.

Scotland

At the news that James II had fled, crowds in Edinburgh broke down the Catholic furnishings at the royal chapel in Holyrood House, but the assumption of power by William and Mary in Scotland was a much less clearly defined event than it was in England. One historian of the period avers that 'The Revolution was made in England and imported to Scotland' (Donaldson, 1978, p. 383).

A Convention of Estates was called in March 1689, and initially neither Jacobites nor Williamites commanded a majority. William assured the convention of his desire to secure Protestantism, while James issued threats to those who forsook allegiance to him, thus turning many waverers towards William. William and Mary were declared monarchs in April and accepted the Claim of Right, though its status as a constitutional document was open to question. The different priorities of Scotland and England can be summed up in the differences between the Scottish Claim of Right and the English Bill of Rights. Both documents were drawn up by assemblies of peers and commons and have many similarities, and there are identical passages in them. But the differences between the concerns of the two countries become apparent when we look at the list of complaints against King James (see Table 12.1).

Table 12.1   Complaints made against James II and VII in the Bill of Rights and the Claim of Right

	English Bill of Rights	Scottish Claim of Right
1	By assuming and exercising a power of dispensing with and suspending of laws, and the execution of laws, without consent of parliament	By erecting public schools, and societies of Jesuits; and not only allowing mass to be publicly said, but also inverting [converting] Protestant chapels and churches to public mass houses, contrary to the express laws against saying and hearing of mass
2	By committing and prosecuting divers worthy prelates, for humbly petitioning to be excused concurring to the said assumed power	By allowing popish books to be printed, and dispersed, by a gift to a popish printer; designing him printer to his Majesty's household, college and chapel, contrary to the law
3	By issuing and causing to be executed a commission under the great seal for erecting a court called, The court of commissioners for ecclesiastical causes.	By taking children of Protestant noblemen and gentlemen, sending and keeping them abroad, to be bred papists ... bestowing pensions upon priests, and perverting Protestants from their religion, by offers of places, preferments and pensions
4	By levying money for and to the use of the crown, by pretence of prerogative, for other time, and in other manner, than the same was granted by parliament	By disarming Protestants, while at the same time he employed papists, in the places of greatest trust, civil and military, such as Chancellor, Secretaries, Privy Councillors, and Lords of Session, thrusting out Protestants, to make room for papists, and entrusting the forts and magazines of the kingdom in their hands
5	By raising and keeping a standing army within this kingdom on time of peace, without consent of parliament, and quartering soldiers contrary to law	By imposing oaths contrary to law
6	By causing several good subjects, being Protestant, to be disarmed, at the same time when papists were both armed and employed, contrary to law	By giving gifts and grants for exacting money, without consent of parliament, or Convention of Estates
7	By violating the freedom of election of members to serve in parliament	By levying, or keeping on foot, a standing army in time of peace, without consent of parliament, which army did exact locality, free and dry quarters
8	By prosecutions in the court of King's Bench, for matters and causes cognizable only in parliament; and by divers other arbitrary and illegal courses	By employing the officers of the army, as judges through the kingdom, and by imposing them where there were heritable [feudal] offices and jurisdictions, by whom many of the lieges were put to death summarily, without legal trial, jury or record

9	And whereas of late years, partial, corrupt, and unqualified persons have been returned and served on juries in trials and particularly divers jurors in trials for high treason, which were not freeholders	By imposing exorbitant fines, to the values of parties' estates, exacting extravagant bail, and disposing fines and forfaultures [forfeitures] before any process or conviction
10	And excessive bail hath been required of persons committed in criminal cases, to elude the benefit of the laws made for the liberty of the subjects	By imprisoning persons without expressing the reason, and delaying to put them on trial
11	And excessive fines have been imposed; and illegal and cruel punishments inflicted	By causing pursue and forfault [forfeit] several persons upon stretches of old and obsolete laws, upon frivolous and weak pretences, upon lame and defective probations, as particularly the earl of Argyll, to the scandal and reproach of the justice of the nation
12	And several grants and promises made of fines and forfeitures, before any conviction or judgement against the persons, upon whom the same were to be levied	By subverting the right of the royal burghs, the third estate of parliament, imposing upon them not only magistrates, but also the whole town council, and clerks, contrary to their liberties ... so that the commissioners to parliament, being chosen by the magistrates and council, the king might well in effect nominate that entire estate of parliament; and many of the said magistrates put in by him, were avowed papists ...
		By sending letters to the chief court of justice, not only ordaining the judges to stop and desist *sine die* [until further notice] to determine causes, but also ordering and commanding them how to proceed, in cases depending before them, contrary to the express laws, and by changing the nature of the judges gifts *ad vitam aut culpam* [for life or for cause], and giving them commissions *ad bene placitum* [at pleasure], to dispose them to compliance and arbitrary courses, and turning them out of their offices when they did not comply
		By granting personal protection for civil debts contrary to law

All of which are utterly and directly contrary to the known laws, statutes and freedoms of this realm

(Sources: Williams, 1960, pp. 26–27; *The Declaration of the Estates of the Kingdom of Scotland Containing the Claim of Right, and the Offer of the Crown to Their Majesties, King William and Queen Mary*, 1689, Edinburgh, pp. 3–4)

EXERCISE

Look at the list of complaints made against the king in Table 12.1 (I have retained the order of the original documents so you may find that the same complaints appear in both documents but in different places). What can we learn about the different priorities of the two nations?

Spend about 20 minutes on this exercise.

SPECIMEN ANSWER

The Scottish document gives greatest emphasis to James's crimes against Protestantism, while the English document focuses much more on his violation of the law and infringement of parliament's powers.

DISCUSSION It is possible that the Scottish parliament gave rise to less passion because it was less powerful than the parliament of England. It would appear from the emphasis in the Scottish list given to the law courts and judges that they were a more important guarantee of subjects' freedoms than parliament. What we don't learn from this list is what constitutional terms were actually agreed on.

Support for the king came from Scottish bishops, who realised that without him their future was doomed. But the Scottish episcopate had come to represent arbitrary royal rule in a way quite unlike their English counterparts. James also had the support of his loyal servant Viscount Dundee and his Highland army. Dundee was killed at the battle of Killiecrankie, though his force was victorious there. His troops staggered on for a bit, without much verve, but the presence of such military opposition made it necessary for William to keep the Scottish parliament loyal to vote money to allow a royal army to be maintained in Scotland. The final act in the suppression of the rebellious Highlanders, a spectacular propaganda failure, was the massacre of Glencoe in which thirty-eight Highlanders were killed by William's military forces, whom they had accommodated for the past fortnight.

Ireland

James's flight to France and Louis XIV's offer of help with an invasion of Ireland immediately made the conquest of Ireland an imperative in William's European policy. James landed in Ireland in March 1689; the English navy failed to prevent this and a later force from landing.

Derry, having become the main centre of Protestant resistance, needed to be subdued, and in April the siege began, effectively a blockade by Catholic troops of a walled city sheltering some 20,000 soldiers and civilians. Three regiments of Protestant troops failed to dislodge the besieging Catholics; finally, on 28 July, the Protestant forces approached the city up the river, and after 105 days the city was relieved.

This episode was rapidly presented as a tale of heroic resistance. The acting governor, a Church of Ireland clergyman, George Walker, travelled to London and was presented to the king after a triumphant progress through Scotland and northern England. While in London, he published an account of the siege that appeared in at least three English editions in 1689, as well as in Scottish, Dutch and German editions. He published other works of Protestant polemic as well (see Figure 12.3).

EXERCISE Read Anthology Document 3.21, 'Extract from George Walker's account of the siege of Derry, 1689'.

1   What effect would such publications as these have (note particularly the dates and places of publication)?

2   How were these effects achieved?

Spend about 30 minutes on this exercise.

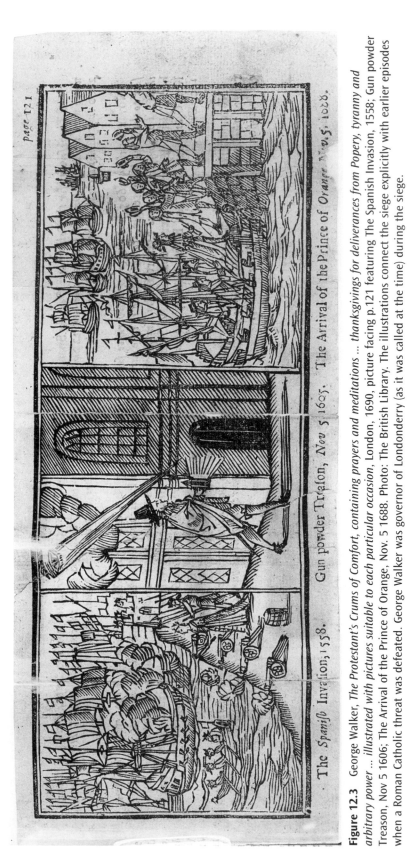

Figure 12.3   George Walker, *The Protestant's Crums of Comfort, containing prayers and meditations ... thanksgivings for deliverances from Popery, tyranny and arbitrary power ... illustrated with pictures suitable to each particular occasion*, London, 1690, picture facing p.121 featuring The Spanish Invasion, 1558; Gun powder Treason, Nov 5 1606; The Arrival of the Prince of Orange, Nov. 5 1688. Photo: The British Library. The illustrations connect the siege explicitly with earlier episodes when a Roman Catholic threat was defeated. George Walker was governor of Londonderry (as it was called at the time) during the siege.

1   Walker was particularly prized as a propagandist in the war against Catholicism: for those who were doubtful about rebelling against the hereditary king, Walker's account assured them of the horrors of the Catholics. The account was rushed out within a few weeks and was published in those places where it might strengthen the Protestant cause. Defeating James was part of the European war against Louis XIV in which William was engaged, hence the publication of editions on the continent where it might be read by anti-French allies.

2   Walker used the form of a diary (we don't know if he had actually kept one in this form). It is the diary details – the gradual diminution in the number of men, the list of unpalatable food with its prices – that provide such a vivid account of the hardships of the besieged population. The account consciously draws on a tradition of anti-Catholic propaganda of a type we saw in Unit 10 in connection with the 1641 rising. He attributes the victory to God and cowardice to the enemy who ran away in the night.

Walker's account was not published in Ireland, and proved to be controversial. A Presbyterian minister, John Mackenzie, who was chaplain to one of the regiments in Derry, published a critique of Walker for taking too much credit for himself and giving not enough to the Presbyterians. Another pamphlet attempted to give credit to Colonel Michelburne as joint commander with Walker, saying of Walker that his 'conduct appeared more conspicuous in the eating part than the fighting, and reason good, the charge of the stores, and provision being committed to him alone' (*An Account*, 1692, 'Epistle to the reader', unpaginated).

Despite the Protestant victory at Derry and success at Enniskillen, the Irish Jacobites held out, so William sent the duke of Schomberg in August 1689 with a force. The two sides were evenly matched, so William arrived himself in June 1690, having sent over a further 7,000 soldiers in advance. James's forces, with French reinforcements, would have matched these had not Louis XIV required that the same number of Irish troops be sent to France. On 1 July, the two armies met in the Boyne Valley, north of Dublin. Anthology Document 3.22, 'A Jacobite account of the battle of the Boyne', is an account of the Jacobite defeat written by an Englishman serving in James's army.

James fled to France on 4 July and William took control of Dublin and eastern Ireland. The siege of Limerick, bravely held by the Catholic forces within, reinvigorated the Jacobites, as did William's return to England, but at the same time the French army left. The war continued into the next year with a crushing defeat of the Jacobites at Aughrim (30 June 1691) and a second siege of Limerick. The Treaty of Limerick (3 October 1691) marked the final surrender of James's armies.

The most striking effects of the Williamite victory were in the intensification of religious divisions and in the land settlement, which continued the work of the early seventeenth-century and Cromwellian transfers of land from Catholics to Protestants. The Treaty of Limerick offered Catholics freedom of worship consistent with the laws of Ireland, or as they had enjoyed in Charles II's reign, and assured the property of Jacobites who took an oath of allegiance to William and remained in Ireland. The penal laws that were eventually enacted were regarded as a breach of faith in that persecution of Catholics intensified. At the same time, Protestants who were not members of the Church of Ireland (chiefly Ulster Presbyterians who were nearly as numerous as Anglicans and whose numbers were growing through emigration from Scotland), were not granted anything comparable to the English Toleration Act. Dissenters were, however, able to vote and sit in the Irish parliament but not in local municipal corporations; but, for the most part, Presbyterians were too poor to be involved in parliament.

James II had allowed Irish Catholics to think that there might be some renegotiation of earlier land settlements. Subsequently, William made some very large grants of land in Ireland to his foreign associates. These were cancelled by the English parliament, an action that caused much annoyance in Ireland, especially to the people who had bought land from the recipients of William's generosity. The Williamite transfer of land was not as extensive as that agreed under the Restoration settlement, but the largest transfers took place in the richest provinces of Leinster and Munster. The effects were compounded by legislation that prevented Catholics from purchasing land or leasing it for more than 31 years. Any land owned by Catholics could only be passed on by inheritance if it was divided equally between all possible male heirs. This had the effect of reducing the size of individual Catholics' property holdings. The effects of this can be seen in Table 12.2.

Table 12.2   Percentage of land owned by Catholics in Ireland

1641	60%
1675	22%
1703	14%

(Sources: Simms, 1978, p. 426; Simms, 1986, p. 12)

The settlement in Ireland was not achieved simply by the Treaty of Limerick but by a sequence of legislation over the succeeding twenty years which assured that: Protestants who had acquired land confiscated from Catholics had secure tenure; members of the Church of Ireland had a monopoly of civil and military offices; only Protestants could sit in the Irish parliament. The Irish House of Commons tried to extend its power as a result of meeting more often to vote taxation for the king, but it did so in the interests only of a very narrow range of people who remained in control of the country for the best part of a century.

RETURN TO THE THEMES

State formation

At various points in this block we have considered what a seventeenth-century state was. Let us now consider what changes took place in the state between the reigns of Charles I and William and Mary, and to what causes we might attribute those changes.

FXFRCISE Look now at Table 12.3 below and, thinking about the comparable tables for the earlier periods (Unit 9, Table 9.1, and Unit 11, Table 11.1), answer the following questions:

1   Were there any changes in the claims of any of the nations to be states?

2   What changes had taken place by 1691?

Spend about 30 minutes on this exercise.

Table 12.3   Changes in England (with Wales), Scotland and Ireland between the reigns of Charles I and William and Mary

	England and Wales	**Scotland**	**Ireland**
Ruler			
Restoration settlement and Charles II	Charles II, 1660–85 (his reign was officially dated from the death of Charles I in 1649). Hereditary succession challenged by attempts from 1679 to make Charles's illegitimate son the duke of Monmouth heir in place of his brother James, duke of York	Charles II declared king in Scotland in 1649 and crowned there 1651, but did not rule until 1660 From 1681, James, duke of York, was king's commissioner in Scotland	Charles II declared king in 1649 but did not rule until 1660 Royal authority was represented by lord lieutenant/lord deputy
James II and VII	James II, 1685–88. James fled, on the strength of which the hereditary succession was set aside to prevent his Catholic son succeeding him	Reigned as James VII	Lord lieutenant/lord deputy Catholic earl of Tyrconnell, 1687–90 James II fled to Ireland in 1689 and remained there until defeated by William III at the Boyne, 1690
William III and Mary and the Revolution settlement	No amendment of constitution required to admit William III and Mary, 1688–1702. Mary had a claim to the throne as daughter of James II, but her husband continued to rule after her death in 1694. After 1689, ideas of contract rather than divine right prevailed. Protestant succession was assured under 1701 Act of Settlement following death of James II in exile and of the son of Anne (nearest Protestant male heir)	Reigned as William II in Scotland	Lord lieutenant/lord deputy Sidney, 1690–95

Legislature

Restoration settlement and Charles II	Parliament meeting at Westminster consisting of House of Lords (peers and bishops) and House of Commons (1 member for each borough and 2 for each county elected by men owning freeholds worth more than 40 shillings/£2). Right to call and dismiss parliament was monarch's alone but limited by 1664 Triennial Act. Charles flouted Act after 1684	Single chamber parliament meeting in Edinburgh consisting of Scottish peers (whose numbers doubled 1603–1707), 14 bishops and burgesses representing burghs (royal burghs increased from 50 to 67). Right to call and dismiss parliament was king's, proceedings dominated by Lords of the Articles (restored 1661). Rival assemblies (such as the Convention of Royal Burghs and the General Assembly of the Kirk) were also able to legislate. 1661 Act Recissory rescinded all legislation since 1633. Parliament began to operate more as a debating chamber and less as a place to approve reports of Committee of Articles	Parliament meeting in Dublin consisting of House of Lords (peers and bishops) and House of Commons. From 1661, Commons exclusively Protestant. Right to call and dismiss parliament was lord lieutenant's.
James II and VII	Inherited compliant parliament because of changes made in Charles II's last years	In 1686, James asked parliament to set aside civil disabilities for Catholics	James II, after fleeing England, called a Catholic parliament in Dublin, which sat May–July 1689 and declared all English legislation to be inapplicable to Ireland but did not repeal Poyning's Law
William III and Mary and the Revolution settlement	Convention met Triennial Act 1694 required meetings of parliament every 3 years. After 1707, members for Scottish constituencies sat in Commons and a selected number of Scottish peers in the Lords.	Convention of Estates met in 1689 Committee of Articles abolished in 1689, reducing crown's ability to manage parliament. Bishops excluded in 1689. Scottish parliament abolished in 1707	William's parliaments met more frequently and voted supply more often. Membership restricted to Protestants from 1691, but Catholics could vote in elections. By 1725, 9 of 127 lay peers were Catholic

Judiciary

Restoration settlement and Charles II	Judges appointed at king's pleasure. Church courts restored but used much less. Habeas Corpus Amendment Act 1679	Judges appointed at king's pleasure. Patchwork of ancient local courts, many dependent on landlords	Judges appointed at king's pleasure
James II and VII	Dismissed judges at pleasure. Appointed Catholics to the bench		Appointed 3 Catholic judges
William III and Mary and the Revolution settlement	1691, opposition to royal control of judiciary		

Executive

Restoration settlement and Charles II	Privy Council and ministers chosen by king	During process of restoration, executive directed by committee of English Privy Council. After 1660, king controlled all appointments to executive (posts mainly held by aristocrats)	Committee of English Privy Council for Irish Affairs directed administration
James II and VII	Privy Council and ministers chosen by king	Catholics appointed to influential offices	Catholics admitted to municipal corporations and appointed sheriffs
William III and Mary and the Revolution settlement	Privy Council and ministers chosen by king	King controlled appointments	King controlled appointments

Foreign policy

Restoration settlement and Charles II	Directed by king in London	Directed by king in London	Directed by king in London
James II and VII	Directed by king in London	Directed by king in London	Directed by king in London
William III and Mary and the Revolution settlement	William's foreign policy dominated by maintaining anti-French coalition of European states	Foreign policy directed from London	Foreign policy directed from London aimed at preventing Irish Jacobite–French alliance

Defence

Restoration settlement and Charles II	Return to decentralised militia administered in counties. Militia Act 1662 gave crown control of armed forces	Last English troops left in 1662. Small army retained; after 1667, militia controlled by nobility. Private fiefdoms of Highland nobles left alone. King had power to make war and peace and to make all military appointments	Protestant force kept in arms, latterly Protestant dissenters excluded. Catholics served in English forces abroad. Protestant militia for home defence

| James II and VII | James demanded that Catholics be given commissions in the army | Command of Edinburgh Castle given to a Catholic | James gave commissions to Catholic officers; eventually 2/3 of army was Catholic. Catholic earl of Tyrconnell made lieutenant general of Irish army in 1686. Exported 3 Irish regiments to England |
| William III and Mary and the Revolution settlement | 1697, attacks on William's standing army of foreign soldiers. Huguenot troops sent to Ireland. English parliament demanded the disbanding of all foreign troops and any troops in Ireland over the number of 12,000 | James's Irish regiments disbanded | In 1689, Tyrconnell raised a Catholic army to support James, supplemented by troops provided by Louis XIV of France; James arrived |

Taxation

Restoration settlement and Charles II	Parliament voted Charles customs and excise, supplemented by Hearth Tax 1662. Increasing percentage of crown revenues from indirect rather than direct taxation	Taxation regularised. King granted £480,000 per annum for life from customs and excise. Land tax and cess introduced as exceptional measures for military purposes	King granted customs and external excise in perpetuity
James II and VII			Granted excise in perpetuity
William III and Mary and the Revolution settlement	Parliament declined to vote William and Mary an income sufficient to rule without parliament. Taxation rose to pay for the wars with France, leading to a financial revolution and the creation of the National Debt in 1693	Parliament experimented with new taxes: poll tax 1693, 1695, 1698; hearth tax 1690; cess at raised level	In 1689, James's Catholic parliament granted him £20,000 a month for 13 months

Church

Restoration settlement and Charles II	Bishops and Church of England parish organisation and liturgy restored in 1660. In 1662, all ministers required to take Act of Uniformity; 2,000 ministers (about 10 per cent) declined to be part of the Church of England. Nonconformists persecuted under the terms of the Clarendon Code. In 1662 and 1672, Charles issued Declaration of Indulgence suspending the operation of laws that forbade Catholic or nonconformist worship: both were withdrawn. Test Act 1673 excluded Catholics and Protestant non-conformists from holding elected or civic office	Bishops restored in 1661, appointed by king. Main administration of church remained with the General Assembly and with the hierarchy of assemblies down to parish level (kirk sessions). 1662 statutes revived lay patronage, declared covenants unlawful, forbade private conventicles 270 Covenanting ministers (about 25 per cent of the total) refused to accept church settlement in 1663 From 1669, indulgence allowed limited toleration of milder Covenanters 1670, preaching at conventicles made a capital offence 1672, 2nd indulgence 1681, Test Act	Bishops and Church of Ireland parish organisation and liturgy restored in 1660
James II and VII	Issued Declarations of Indulgence in 1687 and 1688.	Parliament declined to agree to set aside civil disabilities for Catholics In 1686, James declared freedom of worship for Catholics and Quakers by prerogative 1687, Declaration of Indulgence for Catholics, Quakers and Presbyterians	Church of Ireland remained unmolested but James made no appointments; Catholic bishops allowed to appear in public in clerical dress; Catholic schools and convents established; Church of Ireland revenues used to subsidise Catholic bishops

Church (contd)

| William III and Mary and the Revolution settlement | 400 Anglican clergy (non-jurors) refused to swear oath of allegiance to William and Mary 1689 Toleration Act permitted freedom of worship to Protestant dissenters but not to Catholics or Unitarians. Only Anglicans could attend university or hold elected or civic offices | In 1690, William accepted Scottish demands to re-establish Presbyterian church without bishops. Though Presbyterianism was restored, the covenants were not 152 ministers deprived in 1689 for supporting episcopacy In 1690, General Assembly met for first time since 1653; from 1694, it regulated its own business and meetings | Only 1 non-juring Church of Ireland bishop Church of Ireland in bad state with churches in disrepair and few effective clergy Presbyterians in Ulster increased by immigrants from Scotland 1695, 1st of penal laws against Catholics, prohibiting Catholics from education, carrying arms, or owning a horse worth more than £5 In 1697, Catholic bishops and regular clergy banished. Parish clergy had to register under law of 1704 |

SPECIMEN ANSWER

1   During the period 1649–60, Scotland and Ireland had been absorbed into a single British state. But before that and after that neither had been able to operate entirely as sovereign states. Within the three kingdoms, the relationship between monarch, executive and legislature had varied over the period. Neither the Scottish nor the Irish parliament had been able to assume as much control over the monarch as the English parliament had, but the monarch retained a number of important powers:
   - the right to dispense individuals from the law (but not to suspend the laws)
   - the right to summon and dissolve parliament (subject to the Triennial Acts)
   - the right to appoint councillors and judges.

2   By 1691, it was quite clear that the monarch was under the law and that the basis of his/her relationship with his/her subjects was that of contract rather than divine right. One important change that affected the monarch's relations with each of the three nations was the escalating cost of government. Even without warfare, ordinary administration was impossible without grants of taxation from parliament. This inevitably subjected royal policy to greater scrutiny.

If monarchs had had to give up claims to divine right, it did not mean that they assented willingly to a diminution of their powers. All the monarchs tested the extent of their powers, some with more impunity than others. Even Charles II flouted the Triennial Act and William had an extensive dispute over the maintenance of a standing army in peacetime in defiance of the Bill of Rights. The state in 1691 was not one in which the people had unequivocally triumphed.

In Unit 9, we looked briefly at the views of the historian Jonathan Scott in relation to the question of religion in early modern states. But in fact his most pungent comments concern the role of warfare in state building.

> What eventually created the British state ... [was] the transformation of English military power ... the result most importantly not of Anglo-Scots, or -Irish but Anglo-Dutch collaboration.
>
> (Scott, 2000, p. 16)

> For Charles I war, the sport of princes, was essential to monarchical power. For William monarchical power was essential to war. Accordingly the constitutional changes of 1689–1701, while securing parliaments, also recovered, after a century of disaster, the military substance of English monarchy. This parliamentary monarchy was the centre-piece of the newly constructed English state. It was thus in the context of this military struggle that there occurred all those constitutional alterations which amounted to the creation of a strong parliamentary monarchy.
>
> (Scott, 2000, p. 483)

Scott places the development of the state firmly in the context of European wars and it was European wars that tested the king's powers to make foreign policy, to raise armies and to levy taxation. But it was the Civil Wars in England and the wars in Scotland and Ireland that actually resulted in the existence, for a brief period, of a centralised unitary state with extensive powers of taxation, with a substantial army and security machine. Though it was hated, the English population put up with it without violent demur for a surprisingly long time.

Beliefs and ideologies

Although Scott hangs his argument for the development of the English state on warfare, he also offers the view that Britain was a multiple monarchy with partially reformed religion, not unlike the Habsburg monarchy.

> The crisis of 1618–48 threw not only the whole of religiously mixed, half-reformed central and western Europe into conflict, but Britain too, because Britain was part of religiously mixed, half-reformed central and western Europe.
>
> (Scott, 2000, p. 28)

In Unit 9, we also looked at the view of the historian John Morrill that the English Civil War was not the first European revolution but the last of the European wars of religion. He takes the view that:

> The localist and the legal-constitutionalist perceptions of misgovernment lacked the momentum, the passion, to bring about the kind of civil war which England experienced in 1642. It was the force of religion that drove minorities to fight, and forced majorities to make reluctant choices.
>
> (Morrill 1993 [1984], p. 47)

How would you characterise differences of approach of the two historians?

Spend about 10 minutes on this exercise.

Scott sees Britain as part of a wider European pattern, resembling other European states in spread of religious belief and in the significance of warfare for state building. Morrill, by contrast, regards Europe as offering a basis for comparison, but believes that it was essentially internal religious differences that drove people to war.

Both are concerned with the nature of the state and with its relation to religious beliefs and ideologies, and both see the role of religion as, to some extent, unfinished business. Morrill looks backward, seeing the War of the Three Kingdoms as the last of a sequence of events determined by the Reformation, while Scott looks forward, to the inception of a British (as opposed to English) state and to the forces that created it. Scott is concerned to argue that war created the English state that was a necessary precondition for the British state, but does not offer here any particular explanation for the start of the Civil Wars in England. (Indeed, elsewhere he comments that the question 'What were the causes of the Civil War?' is misposed.)

Producers, consumers and the economy

We saw in Unit 11 something of the effect of the Civil Wars on local manufacturing and consumption. But during the period, foreign trade became of increasing importance. The separate nations of the British Isles did not share a customs union, so there were customs dues to pay on goods transported between the three kingdoms. It was over this period that England's economic predominance was confirmed. England was larger, richer and more populous, and had better developed industry and agriculture, and a succession of Acts gave England control of most of the foreign trade. The 1660 Navigation Act and the Irish Cattle Acts inhibited the trade of Scotland and Ireland to protect that of England.

The most important changes in the economy took place shortly after the period when this block properly ends: the creation of the national debt and the Bank of England in 1694. These were both direct consequences of William's wars with France, and in turn they led to the financial revolution that created the stock market and modern banking.

WHAT WAS THE REVOLUTION?

It is hard in these post-Marxian days to understand how passionately the debate about the revolutionary nature of the English Civil War was conducted in the 1960s and 1970s. The outstanding historian of the Civil War period was Christopher Hill (1912–2003). Although he concluded that 'the English revolution ended in a sordid compromise' (quoted in George, 1988, p. 18), he insisted that it was the events of the 1640s and not those of the 1680s that shaped English society by creating the institutions that allowed for the emergence of a capitalist class by doing away with the relics of feudalism. Such a view is not confined to Marxists. There are other historians who see in the events of the 1640s and 1650s the beginnings of the institutions and values of a modern state and society, even if they do not subscribe to a class analysis.

We could argue that the real revolution took place not in the 1640s but in the 1650s, when a republic was established, a parliament sat with a much enlarged franchise and power over the head of state, and there was limited religious toleration for Protestants. Scotland and Ireland were simply dragged along in the train of these developments. But the failure of these experiments and the constant reversion to the power of the military suggest that there was no group whose interests were really served by such a revolution that extended the state's powers. In the 1650s, the Protestant population of England, while allowed to worship more or less freely and with fewer controls on speech and the press than had been in place in the 1630s, was far more heavily taxed than it had been before the war, and the executive was far more centralised than previously.

The idea that it was the 1680s that constituted the real revolution has been associated with what is known as the 'Whig view of history'. At its most basic, this is the idea that the events of the past are moving inexorably towards a better, freer and more democratic society and that the Revolution of 1688 secured the first steps towards religious toleration, freedom of speech, the supremacy of parliament and restrictions on the powers of the monarch. One of its most fulsome exponents, G.M. Trevelyan (1876–1962), wrote that while other European states were developing military despotism, England developed a system of government that combines 'freedom with efficiency, and local rights with national union', showing the world by example 'how liberty could mean not weakness but strength' (Trevelyan, 1949 [1904], p. xii).

No one seriously suggests that events in Scotland or Ireland constituted bourgeois revolutions. However, the period of covenanting rule has been construed as revolutionary and certainly between 1638 and 1653 the Covenanters were doing their best to create a confessional state on the basis that the National Covenant was a nationalist manifesto. Although Scottish Presbyterianism was intensely authoritarian, it was also egalitarian. The period of dominance of the Confederation of Kilkenny, by contrast, created an aristocratic, Counter-Reformation confessional state. At its collapse, Ireland became more of a colony then ever before, as the Catholics of all classes were progressively excluded from the country's political life.

Perhaps, apart from the defining moments of King Charles I raising his standard at Nottingham, his execution, and the arrival of William III at Torbay, we can encapsulate the revolutionary changes in the beliefs and ideologies of the period in England in two quotations. The first, from the New Testament, 'For where two or three are gathered together in my name, there am I in the midst of them' (Matthew 18: 20) represents the change that took place in English religion, though not in religion in Scotland and Ireland. The gathered congregations of the 1640s and 1650s who grew into the respectable nonconformist churches of the 1660s and 1670s were finally accepted by the Toleration Act of 1689. This aimed to 'ease scrupulous consciences in the exercise of religion' by excepting certain people (but not 'popish recusants') from the harshest of the Elizabethan statutes requiring attendance at Church of England services. But even this limited toleration was not extended to Protestant dissenters (chiefly Presbyterians) in Ireland. In Scotland, when bishops were abolished in the Church of Scotland, those who left the Church of Scotland because of their belief in the episcopacy lived uneasily with the accusation that they were also supporters of the deposed Stuart monarchy.

The second quotation is from a speech by Colonel Rainsborough at the Putney debates in 1647:

> The poorest he that is in England hath a life to live as the greatest he; and therefore truly, sir, I think it's clear that every man that is to live under a government ought first by his own consent to put himself under that government.
>
> (Aylmer, 1975, p. 100)

While neither 1660 nor 1688 created an enlarged franchise – it was necessary to wait until 1832 for that – the Revolution of 1688 formally confirmed that the monarch ruled under the law and not above it, and that the law was made in parliament. Under the Act for Establishing the Coronation Oath of 1689, the archbishop of Canterbury was instructed to ask the monarch to assent under oath to the question 'Will you solemnly promise and swear to govern the people of the kingdom of England, and the dominions thereunto belonging, *according to the statutes in parliament agreed on, and the laws and customs of the same*?' (my emphasis) (Williams, 1960, p. 37).

CONCLUSION

Back to Mrs King

Let us leave the last word to Frances King, whom you met in Unit 9. Now that we have more or less reached the point from which she was looking back, let us ourselves look through her eyes on the period we have covered in this block.

EXERCISE

Reread Anthology Document 3.3, 'Mrs Frances King's account of the war and its aftermath'. Does Mrs King describe a revolution?

Spend about 30 minutes on this exercise.

SPECIMEN ANSWER

In a way she does. She describes both a civil war in which major political figures appear (Cromwell, the king, lawyers), but also an intensely local dispute in which the sequestrators were people who had worked for her father. These were little people who had suddenly acquired power and exercised it in a mean and vindictive fashion over the clergyman's family. Great events and the theft of dinner or a playground fight are all mixed up together.

DISCUSSION

While reading this document it is important to remember when it was written and for what purpose. The author did not personally remember many of the events she recounted, and those she did remember she saw as a child. She was, as an older woman (she must have been at least sixty years of age when she wrote the letter), reporting the stories that had been told in her family about the Civil War and, in particular, about her father's sufferings. So, she was passing on a narrative constructed to make sense of the family's misfortunes. There are a good many similar accounts, though few of them so long and few of them by women. But circumstantial detail is the stuff of these stories and favourite subjects are food, clothing, beds and shelter. Mrs King's account reminds us that civil wars are as much wars about neighbours as about grand ideas.

REFERENCES

An Account of the Transactions in the North of Ireland, Anno Domini, 1691 (1692) London.

Aylmer, G.E. (1975) *The Levellers and the English Revolution*, London, Thames and Hudson.

Donaldson, G. (1978) *Scotland: James V – James VII*, Edinburgh History of Scotland, vol. 3, Edinburgh, Oliver and Boyd.

Evelyn, J. (n.d.) *Diary*, ed. W. Bray, London, Simpkin, Marshall, Hamilton, Kent & co.

Fyfe, J.G. (ed.) (1928) *Scottish Diaries and Memoirs 1550–1746*, Stirling, Eneas Mackay.

George, C.H. (1988) 'Christopher Hill: a profile' in Eley, G. and Hunt, W. (eds) *Reviving the English Revolution: Reflections and Elaborations on the Work of Christopher Hill*, London, Verso.

Jones, J.R. (1978) *Court and Country: England 1658–1714*, London, Edward Arnold.

Morrill, J. (1993) 'The religious context of the English civil war' in *The Nature of the English Revolution*, London, Longman, pp. 45–68. (This essay was first published in *Transactions of the Royal Historical Society*, 5th series, vol. 34, 1984.)

Scott, J. (2000) *England's Troubles: Seventeenth-Century English Political Instability in a European Context*, Cambridge, Cambridge University Press.

Simms, J.G. (1986) 'The establishment of Protestant ascendancy, 1691–1714' in Moody, T.W. and Vaughan, W.E. (eds) *A New History of Ireland*, vol. 4, *Eighteenth-Century Ireland*, Oxford, Clarendon Press, pp. 1–30.

Simms, J.G. (1978) 'The Restoration 1660–85' in Moody, T.W., Martin, F.X. and Byrne, F.J. (eds) *A New History of Ireland*, vol. 3, *Early Modern Ireland 1534–1691*, Oxford, Clarendon Press, pp. 420–53.

Simms, J.G. (1978) 'The war of the two kings 1685–91' in Moody, T.W., Martin, F.X. and Byrne, F.J. (eds) *A New History of Ireland*, vol. 3, *Early Modern Ireland 1534–1691*, Oxford, Clarendon Press, pp. 478–508.

Trevelyan, G.M. (1949 [1904]) *England under the Stuarts*, 29th edn, London, Methuen.

Williams, E.N. (1960) *The Eighteenth-Century Constitution: Documents and Commentary 1688–1815*, Cambridge, Cambridge University Press.

FURTHER READING

Barnard, T. (2004) *The Kingdom of Ireland, 1641–1760*, Basingstoke, Palgrave Macmillan.

Macinnes, A. (2005) *The British Revolution 1629–1660*, Basingstoke, Palgrave Macmillan.

Smith, D.L. (1998) *A History of the Modern British Isles 1603–1707: The Double Crown*, Oxford, Blackwell.

GLOSSARY

Agitators   Representatives elected in 1647 to press the grievances of soldiers in the New Model regiments.

Anglican   Of the Church of England or Church of Ireland. Both churches were headed by the monarch and governed by bishops, and both followed the services specified in the Book of Common Prayer and theology set out in the Thirty-Nine Articles.

Apostolic succession   Belief that bishops were the direct spiritual descendants of Christ's apostles, through the ceremony of the laying on of hands.

Arminian   Supporter of the beliefs published by Jacob Arminius that grace (salvation) could be earned; beliefs favoured by those who rejected the doctrine of predestination.

Assessment   Weekly tax.

Canons   Regulations governing the Church of England and the Church of Ireland.

Church of England   Protestant church founded as a consequence of Henry VIII's breach with the papacy in the 1530s. Its secular head was the monarch, its ecclesiastical head was the archbishop of Canterbury and it was administered by bishops. Until 1689, attendance at its services was enforced by law.

Church of Ireland   Protestant church founded in 1540 after Henry VIII's breach with the papacy in the 1530s. Its secular head was the monarch, its ecclesiastical head was the archbishop of Armagh and it was administered by bishops. Doctrinally similar to the Church of England, but not identical.

Church of Scotland   Protestant church founded in 1560. Its organisation was Presbyterian (by assemblies) and its theology was Calvinist.

Commonwealth   Regime between the execution of the king (1649) and the start of the Protectorate (1653).

Communion   see **Holy Communion**.

Confederate   Of the Irish Catholic Confederation of Kilkenny.

Confederation of Kilkenny   Alliance of Gaelic Irish and Old English who established a Catholic provisional government in Kilkenny from 1642 to 1649.

Conventicle   Illegal religious congregation.

Convention   An assembly resembling parliament but not called by the monarch (called in 1660 and 1688).

Convocation   The governing body of the Church of England.

Covenant   See **Solemn League and Covenant** and **National Covenant**.

Covenanter   Supporter of the Scottish National Covenant.

Debenture   Document guaranteeing the right to an allocation of land in lieu of pay; most commonly used of the scheme to allocate Irish land to pay Cromwellian forces there.

Deposition   Sworn statement.

Diocese   Area of jurisdiction of a bishop.

Dissenter   One who dissented from the Church of England's liturgy and worship; normally used of Protestants after 1660.

Divine right of kings   Belief that the king owed his powers to God and was answerable to God for the protection of his subjects.

Engagement   Alliance between the king and the Scots made in 1647.

Engager   Supporter of Charles I's 'Engagement' with the Covenanting Scots.

Episcopacy   System of church government by bishops.

Episcopate   Body of bishops.

Eucharist   see **Holy Communion**.

Free grace   Doctrine that salvation is not foreordained but given freely by God.

Gaelic Irish   Native Irish, Gaelic-speaking Catholics who retained in the seventeenth century some vestiges of their earlier clan organisation.

General Assembly of the Kirk   Governing body of the Church of Scotland with both clerical and lay members.

Holy Communion   Bread and the wine administered at a communion service to the laity by the minister (Protestant) or the bread administered at the Mass to the laity by the priest, the wine was taken only by the priest (Roman Catholic).

Homilies, Book of   Collection of written addresses used by Anglican clergy who could not preach their own sermons.

Humble Petition and Advice   Revised Protectorate constitution of 1657.

Independent   One who believed in a church based on a voluntary gathered congregation, each being self-sufficient with no organisation beyond the individual congregation.

Instrument of Government   Constitution establishing the Protectorate in 1653.

Interregnum   Interval between kings, usually used of the period 1649–60.

Jacobite   Supporter of the deposed James II and VII, of his son the Old Pretender.

Kilkenny, Confederation of   See **Confederation of Kilkenny**.

Liturgy   Order of service, Anglican liturgy published in Book of Common Prayer.

Minister (of the church)   Functionary appointed either by a bishop (Anglican) or by a congregation (nonconformist) to conduct services and minister to the faithful.

Mortality crisis   Exceptionally raised death rate.

National Covenant   A document stating that changes to the Church of Scotland required the approval of the General Assembly of the Kirk and parliament, and could not be decreed by the king. In February 1638, it was subscribed in Edinburgh and circulated to every burgh and parish for signature.

New English   Protestant Englishmen and women who settled in Ireland from the sixteenth century on.

Nonconformist   One who did not conform to the Anglican Church's liturgy and worship; normally a Protestant.

Old English   Descendants of the twelfth-century Norman invaders of Ireland; predominantly Catholic, though some Protestant converts. They dominated the government of Ireland until the mid seventeenth century. Many spoke Irish (Gaelic) and had married into Gaelic Irish families.

Planter   Settler on an allocation of land; usually used of the English and Scots who took up allocations of land confiscated from rebellious Catholic Irish landowners.

Predestinarian   One who believes in predestination.

Predestination   Doctrine that certain individuals are foreordained to salvation. Characteristically Calvinist, a belief held by many orthodox Anglicans before 1642.

Prelacy   System of church government by bishops.

Presbyterian   Believer in a system of church government by a hierarchy of assemblies with lay and clerical members. Often associated with Calvinist doctrine.

Prerogative   Particular power reserved to monarch.

Presbytery   Assembly of lay people and ministers from several parishes charged with administering those parishes.

Priest   Roman Catholic clergyman; used as a term of abuse of ceremonialist Protestant clergy.

Protestor   See **Remonstrant**.

Puritan   Someone who believed that the reform of the Anglican Church had not gone far enough in a Protestant direction; usually used before 1660.

Regicide   Act of killing a king; one of those who signed King Charles I's death warrant.

Remonstrant (or Protester)   Supporter of the Remonstrance (October 1650), which denounced any understanding with Charles II and sought to enforce the Act of Classes.

Resolutioner   Supporter of alliance between moderate Covenanters and royalists.

Solemn League and Covenant   Both the military alliance of 1643 between Scotland and England, *and* the agreement that the English would implement the Scottish system of church government; signed by members of parliament and the parliamentary army.

Subsidy   Direct tax granted to the king by parliament to meet particular occasions.

Tonnage and poundage   Tax on imports granted to the king at his accession by parliament.

Transubstantiation   Roman Catholic belief that the elements (the bread and wine of Holy Communion) were transformed by the miracle of the Mass into the actual body and blood of Christ.

Westminster Assembly of Divines   Assembly established 1643 to devise a new church settlement for England and Wales in accordance with the terms of the Solemn League and Covenant.

INDEX